FACES ABOUT THE CROSS

BOOKS BY THE SAME AUTHOR

SERMONS FROM JOB

MEET THESE MEN

IN PARABLES

THE SEVEN WORDS

ANOINTED TO PREACH

WHEN THE CHURCH WAS YOUNG

LIVING ZESTFULLY

FEMININE FACES

THE ROAD TO CERTAINTY

VALUES THAT LAST

TEN RULES FOR LIVING

SERMONS FROM THE MIRACLES

CHAPPELL'S SPECIAL DAY SERMONS

SERMONS ON THE LORD'S PRAYER

SERMONS FROM THE PARABLES

SERMONS FROM THE PSALMS

THE SERMON ON THE MOUNT

THE VILLAGE TRAGEDY

AND THE PROPHETS

IF I WERE YOUNG

SERMONS FROM REVELATION

QUESTIONS JESUS ASKED

FACES ABOUT THE CROSS

By CLOVIS G. CHAPPELL

ABINGDON PRESS
NEW YORK   NASHVILLE

FACES ABOUT THE CROSS

Copyright MCMXLI by Whitmore & Stone

Library of Congress Catalog Card Number: 41-2232

M

SET UP, PRINTED, AND BOUND BY THE
PARTHENON PRESS, AT NASHVILLE,
TENNESSEE, UNITED STATES OF AMERICA

THIS BOOK IS AFFECTIONATELY
DEDICATED
TO MY DEAR FRIENDS
MR. AND MRS. ARTHUR E. MARTIN
OF WASHINGTON, D. C.

CONTENTS

Contents

I

PROLOGUE

THE STEADFAST FACE

*"And it came to pass, when the time was come that
he should be received up, he steadfastly set his face
to go to Jerusalem."*

LUKE 9:51

HERE IS A PICTURE OF THE FACE OF JESUS WITHOUT
which our view of him would be vastly incom-
plete. Fortunately, the Evangelists give varied views
of our Master. All these are helpful in our understanding of him. Let us glance at a few of these
pictures.

1. They show us the Christ of the sunny face. We
cannot read these Gospels without realizing that Jesus
was a man of deep and genuine joy. We can be sure
that his face was about the sunniest that ever looked
out upon this world. This is indicated, in the first

place, by the fact that out of his own experience he could give utterance to the Beatitudes. "Oh, the joy of the poor in spirit!" he sings. "Oh, the blessedness of the meek!" "Oh, the gladness of the merciful!" It was only a heart full of song that could give birth to such glad shouts as these.

Then there was another word that was upon the lips of Jesus again and again. He uttered it in the face of ravages of sin. He uttered it as he himself faced ghastly death. That word was, "Be of good cheer." And we may be sure that the cheer that he commended to others, he possessed himself. He was too sincere for it to have been otherwise. If such were not the case, his appeal would have counted for little or nothing. How futile for one to call "Courage" to his brother when his own face has gone white and his own knees are buckling under him with fear! We may therefore be sure that the Christ who called "Good cheer" to his frightened friends possessed that cheer himself in superb abundance. In fact, that cheer was so real and full that in his last prayer, he makes this request, "that they might have my joy fulfilled in themselves."

2. Then the face of Jesus is a vivid and vital face. The impression that he made upon those of his day was that of a man who was tremendously alive. Did you ever notice how constantly men were asking him about life? They came to him with that question because they were sure that he knew the answer; that he

knew it, not theoretically simply, but practically. He was really living. One day, for instance, a young aristocrat forgot his superior social standing, forgot the staring eyes of the crowd, to run and fall on his knees before this Carpenter. Thus kneeling, he put to him this question, "Good Master, what good thing shall I do, that I may have eternal life?"

Here is another picture equally impressive. Jesus is preaching to a vast and enthusiastic audience. But he sees that this enthusiasm is largely the result of their having misunderstood his mission. Regardless of the cost, therefore, he resolves to make them understand. He succeeds so thoroughly that they become offended. They begin to leave, first in groups of twos and threes, then by dozens and scores. By and by there is such a mass movement that only twelve are left. These look over their shoulders at the vanishing crowd, with frightened eyes. They are wondering if it would not be the part of wisdom for them to go also. Then Jesus breaks in upon their feverish fears with a quiet question. "Will ye also go away?" Simon Peter starts, blushes, then gives the wisest possible answer. "To whom shall we go? Thou hast the words of eternal life." "We would leave," he seems to say, "but for the fact that we are eager to live, and we are sure that you have the secret of life." The face of Jesus is a vital face.

3. Then the Gospels show us the Christ of the tender face. This is the picture that, above all others, has

gripped the hearts of men. Here is one who will not break the bruised reed, nor quench the smoking flax. His is a tenderness that drew to him outcasts who dared not approach any other. It also drew little children who found his arms more inviting than the arms of their own mothers. It is this gentle and tender Christ that has laid the most compelling grip upon the great painters. In fact, in seeking to emphasize this tenderness, I think they have given us a wrong conception. The face that looks out upon us from the canvas is indeed a very gentle and tender face. It is the face of a man who could love and suffer. But we cannot but feel that something is lacking. That something is rugged strength and courage. It is a high-hearted gallantry that could not only patiently bear, but aggressively dare.

4. For this reason, we need the picture presented by our text. Here is the Christ of the steadfast face. "He steadfastly set his face to go to Jerusalem." Here is a man who can make up his mind. Here is one who, though confronted by deadly dangers, can reach a wholehearted decision. Here is a face so majestic in its strength and purpose that it strikes a holy awe into the hearts of all who have eyes to see. The friends of Jesus were a rather garrulous lot. They were given to much noisy discussion. But as they look upon this steadfast face, Mark tells us that for once they are awed to silence. "Hush!" they whisper one to another. They dare not speak to him. They dare not even walk

at his side. While they lag behind in awe and wonder, he strides on alone, his face set toward Jerusalem.

There is no adequate picture of Jesus that fails to take into consideration this steadfast face. By this I do not mean that here alone we see Jesus as a man of tremendous courage and strength. Such is not the case. The constant impression that he made upon those who knew him was that of a man of vast strength. Wherever he went, the ground fairly shook under the tread of the multitudes that dogged his steps. He stirred his nation as only a strong man could stir it. Even his enemies proclaim his strength by the intensity of their hatred of him. It has been wisely said that we do not hate weaklings. We may ignore or pity or despise them. But we do not hate them. We hate only strong men. The Pharisees hated this Prophet who was turning their world upside down, because he was so strong and daring.

II

Our text brings us face to face with this strength and courage in action. With high resolve Jesus is going to Jerusalem. Only a strong and brave man would have done that under the circumstances. No weakling, knowing what Jesus knew, would have taken this course.

1. This is the case because Jesus knew that at Jerusalem he would meet opposition from the bitterest of enemies. Here he would face implacable foes who

would do anything in their power to destroy him. What made this opposition the harder to bear was the fact that these foes were the religious leaders of the day. They were men upon whose support he had a right to count. Yet they fought him with deadly fury. They hounded him. They sought to entrap him. They endeavored by every means, fair or foul, to discredit and destroy him.

Such opposition is hard to bear. It takes superlative strength and courage not to be disheartened or soured by it. Some of us realize that by appealing to our own experiences. How easily we are turned aside! I went to see a man sometime ago who was nearing the end of his journey. He told me that he had once been an official in his church, the superintendent of his church school, in fact. He had set out to accomplish what he was sure was a worthy purpose, but he met opposition. Not only so, but the one who opposed him was his pastor. It was too much. He quit, and for twenty years he had counted for nothing in the cause that he really loved. He had once thought that he had a good reason, but now he had discovered his mistake. In fact, we never quit because of opposition of the bitterest of foes.

2. In going to Jerusalem, not only did Jesus have to meet the opposition of his enemies, but also of his friends. He had to grieve and disappoint those who loved him best. That was harder than facing his foes. He tried to soften the blow for these friends by telling

them that it was expedient for them that he go away. But they could not understand. They all felt just as Simon did when, after that first disclosure of the Cross, he turned upon his Master and said, "Be it far from thee, Lord!" Jesus knew that it was love that prompted Simon's opposition. But this devotion made the heroic course of Jesus all the more difficult. Therefore he had to say to this friend, "You are a hindrance to me."

We find a similar picture in the life of Paul. He, too, is on his way to Jerusalem. His friends are sure that such a course will get him into trouble. Therefore they gather about him and urge him not to go. But this gallant and battle-scarred hero has come to share the spirit of his Master. Therefore he refuses to listen to their appeal. At last he gets a view of their faces and finds them wet with tears. That is almost more than he can bear. "What do you mean?" he cries as he chokes back his own sobs—"what do you mean by weeping and breaking my heart? I am ready not to be bound only, but also to die at Jerusalem for the name of the Lord Jesus." But his friends made an already hard duty far harder.

3. Not only was it hard for Jesus to go to Jerusalem because of the opposition both of his enemies and of his friends, but because he knew that there he would have to face disaster. I am not saying that Jesus had a blueprint of everything that was to happen. But I am sure of this, that he knew that at Jerusalem he was going to be called upon to face the hard ordeal of the

Cross. Such an ordeal could not but be unspeakably terrible to a fine, sensitive soul like Jesus. The criticism has been offered that Jesus did not meet his crucifixion with the sturdy stoicism that has characterized many a criminal. That is true. But these criminals were not possessed of his sensitiveness. I have called your attention more than once to the fact that as we rise in the scale of being, that rise is marked by an increased capacity for pain. Jesus was supremely great; therefore he had a supreme capacity for suffering. How sublime, therefore, the heroism that enabled him to go to Jerusalem to endure the Cross.

III

Why, then, did Jesus make this unwelcome journey? Why did he steadfastly set his face to go to Jerusalem?

Let us be very sure of this fact, that he went to Jerusalem of his own free will. He did not have to go. He made up his own mind to go. He went as a matter of choice. There was no outward compulsion. If there is one fact upon which Evangelists insist, it is this—that the death of Jesus was voluntary. He was no helpless victim. He himself declared emphatically that his life was not wrenched from his grudging fingers. "No man taketh it from me, but I lay it down of myself. I have power to lay it down, and I have power to take it again." He went to Jerusalem and to the Cross because he chose to do so. But why did he thus choose?

1. He did so because he thought that such was the will of God. Jesus had one supreme purpose in life. That he emphasized over and over again. His purpose was to do the will of God. "My meat," he says, "is to do the will of God and to finish his work. . . . I came not to do mine own will, but the will of him that sent me." There were times when he was perplexed as to what the will of God was. Such was the case in Gethsemane. It was hard for him to believe that his Father willed that he should suffer the pangs of the Cross. At times he was half persuaded that he had misunderstood. Therefore he prayed, "If it be possible, let this cup pass from me."

But while he was at times perplexed to know the will of his Father, he was never in the slightest doubt as to the rightness of that will. Nor was he ever in the slightest degree unwilling to perform it. Believing in the love of his Father, believing in the wisdom of his Father, he was sure that such a wise and loving Friend could will only what was best. Therefore, while at times a bit bewildered and shrinking, he always kept this yearning uppermost in his heart, "Not my will, but thine be done." Jesus steadfastly set his face to go to Jerusalem because he believed that in no other way could he be obedient to the will of God.

2. He set his face steadfastly to go to Jerusalem because he loved Jerusalem. Yes, and because he loved you and me. This city, in spite of its past and future rejection of him, had a secure place in his heart. He

had great dreams for it that he refused wholly to surrender. There is no measuring the yearning love back
of this heart-cry "O Jerusalem, Jerusalem, thou that
killest the prophets, and stonest them which are sent
unto thee, how often would I have gathered thy children together, even as a hen gathereth her chickens
under her wings, and ye would not!" Though they
might refuse what he had to give, he could not take
their refusal as final. His love would not allow him
to do less than his patient and persistent best.

3. Then Jesus set his face steadfastly to go to Jerusalem because he did not believe that his immediate
seeming defeat would be the final word. He was sure
of his coming death, but he was equally sure that his
death would not put a grim, black period to all his
holy hopes. He was not facing this heavy ordeal as
a defeated man. He was not going to Jerusalem as a
victim. He was going as a conqueror. He was sure
that "lifted up from the earth he would draw all men
unto himself." In that mad faith he has not been disappointed. By accepting that Cross Jesus has remade,
and is still remaking, the world. It is Christ crucified
that has been the supreme magnet of mankind through
the centuries. He is so still.

Therefore, we thank God that Jesus steadfastly set
his face to go to Jerusalem. But what has all this to
do with you and me? We are separated from that
scene by seas and continents and centuries. The fact
that Jesus went to Jerusalem in the long ago ought to

hearten and strengthen us to go to our Jerusalem. For Jerusalem is not merely a spot on the map; it is not a matter of geography; it is a matter of doing the will of God. We go to Jerusalem when we accept God's plan and purpose for our lives. It is this loyalty to the will of God that is the very sum-total of Christianity. It is Christianity in its beginning. It is Christianity in its course. It is Christianity in its consummation. We can do nothing less than this and be Christian. We can do nothing greater through all eternity!

But such a course is not always easy. As Jesus steadfastly set his face, so we must set ours. Christianity is not a religion that caters to our weakness and cowardice. It is a religion for heroes. "We Christians are not cowards," Paul declares proudly. By no means. There is absolutely nothing that demands a finer courage than to be a genuine disciple of Jesus. It takes courage to begin; it demands courage and strength for every step of the journey. For this reason many of us fail. Lacking courage for such high adventure, some take a halfway course, while others are too timid even to make a wholehearted beginning. Thus they miss the deepest and sweetest secret of human blessedness.

Many years ago Charles G. Finney was preaching in Rochester, New York. Far up in the balcony sat a brilliant and able lawyer. He was chief justice of the court of New York. As he listened to the minister, conviction laid hold upon his heart. "That man is speaking the truth," he said to himself. "I ought to act upon it. Here and now I ought to make a public confession of Jesus Christ." But there was another voice that spoke, reminding him of the prominent position he held, also how humiliating it would be for him to go forward and make his confession just as any ordinary sinner. "But why not?" came the more manly voice. Then, lest his cowardice might get the better of him, while the minister was still speaking, he arose and went down the stairway and the long aisle. He stepped into the pulpit, plucked the minister by the sleeve, and said, "If you will call for decisions for Christ now, I am ready to come." By that courageous decision he not only found Christ for himself, but was the means of helping to bring a new spiritual springtime to his entire city. God grant this day that you and I might renew our vows and again steadfastly set our faces to go to Jerusalem.

II

A NAMELESS HERO

"One of them ran forthwith, and filling a sponge with sour wine put it on the end of a cane and offered it him to drink; while the rest said, Stay! Let us see whether Elijah is coming to deliver him."

MATTHEW 27:48, 49 (Weymouth)

HERE IS A GROUP OF SOLDIERS GATHERED ABOUT three crosses. These soldiers have finished the real work of the day in that they have already nailed their victims each to his respective cross. They have now only to wait for these doomed men to die. Thus they loll about in their blood-flecked garments trying to while away the tedious hours as best they can. Death by crucifixion is such a slow-footed monster that they are getting genuinely bored. Four of them amuse themselves for a little while by gambling for the seamless robe of the Man they have just crucified. This done, however, there is nothing for them to do, as for the others, but to wait. While they are thus waiting they are startled by this wild cry that comes from the Victim on the middle cross: "Eli, Eli, lama sabachthani."

These soldiers were all alike in that they heard this cry of agony. They were alike in that they did not fully understand just what was being said. Jesus was not speaking in Latin. He was using what to these soldiers was a foreign tongue. He seemed to be calling on a man named Elijah. But while they did not understand it fully, they all alike knew that this was a cry born of suffering. They all realized that it was a pathetic hand reaching out into the encircling gloom for help. But here their likeness ends. While all heard, while all had a partial understanding of its meaning, they differed in this, that they did not make the same response. This tragic cry divided them into two distinct groups. There was one who sought to help, while the others did nothing. This one became a part of the remedy, while the others remained a part of the disease.

I

Naturally we realize that there is that in this scene that is altogether unique. We are dealing here with a historic fact. This is the story of an event that took place at a certain date, and upon a certain hill. This cry of Jesus, "My God, my God, why hast thou forsaken me?" is a cry that none ever uttered just as he uttered it. But while there is that which is unique in the scene, there is also that which is eternal and abiding.

1. There is this bitter cry of pain. This wail of anguish on the part of Jesus is as old as human suffering and as new as the tragedy of today. For, be the causes what they may, humanity is constantly being nailed to some kind of cross. Just why this is the case we are not arguing now; we are merely asserting the fact. Look where you will, in any age, and you will see pathetic hands outstretched for help. Listen upon any day of human history and you will hear the cry of suffering men and women. This cry belongs not to one day, but to every day. It comes with peculiar intensity in your day and mine. But always it is present. It has sobbed its way through the centuries.

2. Not only does this cry of suffering need belong to every day, but it makes itself heard by every man. Of course, some hear it with more sensitive ears than others. Some are more deeply stirred by it than others. But stop our ears how me may, we cannot become completely deaf to it. Again and again it breaks by our complacency, our love of ease, our indifference, to disturb us. Thus disturbed, we make our varied responses, even as these soldiers of the long ago. We hear this call of need whether we will it or not. That is not optional. The one thing that is optional is what we do about it. Thus there are two factors in this scene that abide. There is the cry of anguished need and those who are compelled to hear that cry and to

make some kind of response. So it was on Calvary. So it is today.

II

Let us look at these groups. Some of these soldiers said, "Stay! let us see." How harmless it sounds! They did not rebuke Jesus for his outcry. They did not add to his anguish by any personal violence. They did not even say, "Never under any circumstances are we going to help." They simply said, "We are not going to do anything now." They answered in these familiar words: "Stay! let us see if Elijah will come to save him." Of course they could have given some wise reasons for their conduct, even as you and I. "Why don't you do something?" I asked one of them desperately. His answer is very simple. He has three good reasons:

"I do not do anything, in the first place," he said, "because my name is not Elijah. Didn't you hear what he said? He was not calling on me, for help; he was calling on a chap named Elijah. Since that is the case, helping is none of my business." But there he was altogether wrong. When we come face to face with something that needs to be done that we can help to do, that is a call to us. It is just as genuine a call as if God had written our name in letters of fire across the sky. Yet, we go from generation to generation making the same lame excuses as this soldier.

"I saw the need," we confess, "but it was none of

my business. Oh yes, I saw that your house was on fire. I knew that your child was asleep in that house and would likely be burned to death, but I did nothing; I am no fireman. Yes, I passed down the highway and saw that the bridge was out. But I said nothing about it; I do not belong to the police patrol. Certainly I knew the man was hungry, but I did not feed him; I am not the Community Chest. I knew he was hungry for the Bread of Life, but I did not help him; I am not a minister. I do not even belong to the Church. Certainly, I saw the man that had been robbed and was slowly bleeding to death by the roadside. But I did nothing about it; I am no physician." But when you see a need that you can help in any fashion to meet, God is then and there calling your name.

"But," says this soldier, "I have another reason for not helping. I heard the cry. I knew that the need was desperate. But I had enough confidence in my fellows to believe that somebody else would respond. I could not bring myself to the conviction that there was no man that would do anything. So I waited in the hope that Elijah or someone else would take the matter seriously. I wanted the job done all right. But I thought that if I waited long enough somebody else would do it, then I would not have to be bothered." So we say, "I knew the class ought to be taught; I knew the gift ought to be made; I knew that the bill had to be paid; but I thought if I fumbled in my pocket long enough another would pay and I would be that

25

much to the good. You see I never ask, 'How much can I do,' but only, 'With how little can I get by?' "

There is yet a third reason that this soldier might have given. It is one that is more compelling, I think, than any of the others. "You heard the cry," I repeat, "why didn't you help?" "I wanted to," came the answer, "but the situation seemed utterly hopeless. There was so little that I could do. You see, Rome had arrested this Man and had sentenced him to death. By this time the agonies of the cross had almost done their work. There was now so little life left in him that he seemed little better than dead. What good, therefore, could I do? Could I wrest him from Rome, restore him to health, and give him back to his friends?" Certainly not. Therefore, because I could not do everything, I did not do anything.

This same dismal consideration is especially prevalent today. It threatens to lay benumbing and paralyzing hands on every one of us. Here we are met for worship. While we are thus meeting we realize that after nineteen centuries of Christian preaching and teaching, far more than half the world is at this very moment on fire. In the face of such widespread tragedy what can you do, what can I do, what can anyone do? To undertake to help to meet such tremendous need seems as futile as trying to still a whole tempest-whipped ocean with one drop of oil. These soldiers might have done nothing because they were hopeless, even as you and I.

But there was one of these soldiers who had a more hopeful reading of things. While others say, "Stay," while others tried to put out the fire of his enthusiasm, he ran and got a sponge, and dipped it into his daily portion of sour wine, put it on a reed, and gave Jesus to drink. He did not know just what this dying man was asking at his hands. But he did know that one of the tortures of crucifixion was the burning thirst that such blood-letting occasioned. Therefore, he shared with Jesus his bit of wine. As I watch him, my heart grows warm to him. I cannot keep from expressing my appreciation and approval. "Good work, Elijah," I call. At this he looks at me with surprise. Then, understanding my mistake, he answers, "My name is not Elijah." "Then why are you giving this Man to drink? It sounded to me as if he were calling Elijah." "So it did to me," he replied, "but you can see well enough that Elijah is not coming. For some reason he has fallen down on the job. Maybe he just couldn't get here. But whatever the reason for his failure, I somehow felt that it was up to me to take his place."

When we hear that, we cannot but look at this man again. He seems well worth knowing. I have a fancy that he belongs among the heroes. There was something that needed to be done, and without waiting to see what others would do, he took it upon himself. He is of that select company that perform deeds that nobody has the right to ask him to do. It is when we thus get under burdens voluntarily, for love's sake, that we come to live in the spirit of the cross.

But when this soldier set out to help, was he not also aware of the impossibility of his task? Did he expect so to follow through as to take Jesus from the cross and restore him to health? Certainly not. He was quite aware that that was beyond his power. But he refused to allow the fact that he could not do everything to prevent him from doing anything. Therefore, though he did not save Jesus from the cross, he rendered him the best service of which he was capable. He soothed the tortures of thirst by sharing with him his portion of wine. Surely this man is vastly worth knowing. I am sorry, therefore, that I do not know his name.

At the close of the first World War each nation of the Allies found among their dead a battered body without a name that they buried amid pomp and ceremony. Each nation erected a monument in honor of this nameless hero, bearing this inscription: TO THE UNKNOWN SOLDIER. Our hero has a right to a monument of that kind. He belongs to that immortal company who were so busy doing the deed that they did not have time to leave us their autographs. I read once a beautiful and fitting eulogy to our nameless helpers. Here is one of them: "What is your name, Soldier?" And he hurries on, saying, "I haven't time to tell you now; I have got to go give a drink to this thirsty Man before he dies." But if we do not have his name, we have the deed. That is all that really matters. Who wrote the twenty-third Psalm? Really nobody knows. Many have supposed that David did. But we do not need to know the author so long as we have the song. For centuries nobody knew the sources of the Nile. But the river gave Egypt life and fertility then just as it does today. How much of the best work is done by men and women who simply put through the task without taking time to leave us their calling cards.

> "Common as the wayside grasses,
>   Ordinary as the soil,
> By the score he daily passes,
>   Going to and from his toil;
> Stranger he to wealth or fame,
> He is only What's-his-name.
>
> "Not for him the glittering glory,
>   Not for him the places high,
> Week by week the same old story,
>   Try and fail, and fail and try;
> All his days seem dull and tame—
> Poor, old, plodding What's-his-name.
>
> "Though to someone else the guerdon,
>   Though but few his worth may know,
> On his shoulders rests the burden
>   Of our progress won so slow;
> Red the road by which we came
> With the blood of What's-his-name."

III

What was the outcome of the differing response made by these men? What is the outcome for ourselves? Does it make any serious difference whether or not we respond to the cry of need? Indeed it does! It makes an immeasurable difference, both for time and for eternity.

Look first at those who said, "Stay, let us see." What did they miss? They missed the privilege of helping. They might have been of service to Jesus in his hour of extremity. But while they did nothing, Jesus died. Something like that is always taking place when we refuse to help. Jesus told the story of a certain rich man who was clothed in purple and fine linen and had a banquet every day. This man was not aggressively cruel. On the contrary he was so kind that when a ragged beggar stationed himself at his gate he did not drive him away. Not only so, but he allowed him to be fed with the scraps from his own table. But this was as far as he would go. He never met the beggar. Thus given only the crumbs, we are not surprised to read that the beggar died. Institutions, causes, men—all these die when we neglect them or feed them only upon crumbs.

But they are not the only ones who die: "The rich man also died." Crumbs have a way of killing him that gives as well as him that receives. Thus these soldiers by refusing to give refused also to live. "But," you say, "the record does not tell us this about these soldiers." No, it does not need to tell us. We know both from the Scriptures and from experience that he that seeketh to save his life shall lose it. When? Where? In some far-off tomorrow? Doubtless, but certainly in the here and now. Wherever we find men and women whose one business in life is to look out for themselves, we find sad, fed-up, disillusioned souls who are not really living.

But this unknown soldier, what of him? Having shared his bit of wine with Jesus, I am confident that he came at once to feel the thrill of real life. In thus serving he has done something far bigger than he realizes. "That was a magnificent deed," I say to him. But he looks uncomfortable and answers: "No, it was very small. It made me hurt on the inside because I could do so little." But in spite of the poor estimate that he put upon his gift, because it was his best, it was rated perfect by him to whom it was given. When he reached life's other side I have an idea that he found himself credited with no lesser deed than the saving of Jesus from the cross.

Why do I say this? Because God judges not as man judges. You and I judge each other by results. Some years ago I entered a newspaper office and saw upon the wall a large placard that fairly shrieked this word: "57 RULES FOR MAKING A SUCCESS." I stopped in my tracks. "Here," I said to myself, "is where I tarry. With fifty-seven fingers pointing the way to success, even I need not miss it." So I read as follows: "First, deliver the goods. Second, It doesn't matter about the other fifty-six." There you have it. ▲We judge by results. Effort, dreams, longings, these do not count. What counts is delivering the goods.

But when God judges, he does not look so much at what is in our hands as at what is in our hearts. For instance, it is easy to guess what was the big dream of David's life. He was a great warrior and a great statesman. At his best, if tradition is true, he was a great poet. But he did not expect to live in the grateful memories of his people because of any of these things. That by which he expected to be remembered was that he had built a temple to the honor of his God. But here he was doomed to disappointment. He was not allowed to build. For this reason I am sure that he came to the close of the day feeling that life had been little better than a failure. But God judged otherwise. Hence he said, "Whereas it was in thine heart to build a house in my name, thou didst well that it was in thine heart." And whereas it was in this nameless hero's heart to save Jesus, he was credited with the deed.

This is a bracing and healing word. I like it because it puts us all on an equal footing. The ordinary man has the same opportunity to do big things for his Lord as the man of genius. "It is not what man does, but what man would do, that exalts him." This does not mean of course that because our gifts are small we can excuse ourselves by merely boasting of how much we would do if our abilities were only equal to those of some talented brother. We often permit ourselves to feel quite virtuous by telling how much we would give if we were only as rich as Croesus, while we do nothing with that which is actually ours. But this is to take a bracing truth and make of it nothing more than a benumbing opiate.

We rejoice that God judges us by what is in our hearts. But what is the test of what we have in our hearts? There is just one real test. It is what we do with what is actually in our hands. Jesus was once so thrilled by the gift of a certain widow that he made her immortal. Of all that have given through the centuries, this woman stands among the greatest. Why so? It was not because she told her friends how much she would give if she were worth a billion. It was because, though she had only two mites, a fraction of a cent, she dared for love's sake to give that. The task of saving our world is big. No one of us can do it alone. But we can all do what this nameless hero did, we can give our best. To do that is victory. To do that is to be assured that one day Jesus will greet us with this welcome word: "Well done, well done."

III

CRITICS AND CRITICISM

"They that passed by reviled him."

MATTHEW 27:39

I

CONSPICUOUS AMONG THE FACES ABOUT THE CROSS is that of the critic. At this we need not be surprised. We meet the critic everywhere. In speaking of critics and criticism, therefore, we are on familiar ground. We are dealing with a subject of universal interest. This is the case for at least two reasons.

1. We are all interested in critics and criticism because all of us are at times criticized. (I use the word "critic" throughout this sermon in its adverse sense.) Of course some are criticized far more abundantly and far more sharply than others. Those who suffer most

from the critics are generally the ones who dare to differ most from their fellows. We criticize those who defy our customs and break our laws. We refuse to tolerate those who fall too far behind the procession. These we tend to crucify as Rome did the robbers who died beside Jesus. But if we criticize those who fall behind, we are often equally hard on those that get too far ahead. If these robbers were criticized and crucified because they were too bad, Jesus was criticized and crucified because he was too good. To be conspicuous in any direction is to meet with abundant criticism.

There is therefore a way by which we can greatly reduce the criticism that we have to face. That is by conforming. We can take the advice of the Preacher in Ecclesiastes and refuse to be either too bad or too good. Ovid tells the story of an ancient father who made a pair of wings for his son. These wings were made of feathers that were stuck together by wax. In instructing the lad on how to use them to the best advantage he warned him against flying too low lest he be endangered from the earth. Nor was he to fly too high lest the sun melt the wax and wreck his wings. "You will go safest in the middle," he concluded. Thus he uttered advice that has been much to the edification of millions of politicans and of others as well. But even a middle course will not avoid criticism altogether. This is true, if for no other reason than for the fact that no man has a universal appeal. However good, bad, or indifferent we may be, there will be those who will not approve.

> "I do not love thee, Dr. Fell,
> The reason why I cannot tell;
> But this alone I know full well,
> I do not love thee, Dr. Fell."

All of us at times play the role of Dr. Fell.

2. We are all interested in critics and criticisms because all of us at times play the role of critic. Some of us do this with kindness and with caution. We have some realization of what a deadly dangerous weapon criticism is. Others criticize recklessly and gleefully and with vast self-assurance. These take an unholy pride in their work. They feel that it is all to their credit that they can see more with their eyes shut than others can with their eyes wide open. They are sure that it is a mark of superiority that they have been assigned the task of criticizing the players rather than of taking part in the game. These declare proudly with Iago, "I am nothing, if not critical." But, be our motives good or bad, there are times when we all dare to assume the difficult and dangerous role of critic.

Nor is such a role necessarily wrong. The right to criticize is a part of our democratic inheritance. In a despotism no such right exists. In Germany Hitler is always right. In the United States we can criticize anybody from the President down. This is as it should be. There may be times, therefore, when it is at once our privilege and duty to criticize and to criticize adversely. This I affirm, not forgetting that Jesus said, "Judge not, that ye be not judged." This is a strong word, but it does not forbid criticism. This I say because he follows this command with a second that makes the exercise of our critical faculties an absolute necessity. "Give not that which is holy unto the dogs," he continues, "neither cast ye your pearls before swine." But how are we to obey this command unless we reach some conclusion as to who is swinish and who is not? Therefore, when Jesus said, "Judge not," he was not forbidding just criticism. He was forbidding faultfinding. He was forbidding us to look for the worst in our fellows instead of the best.

If it is never right to criticize, Jesus himself was seriously at fault. To assume that he went about with a smile of approval for all he met is to go vastly wrong. There were some that he approved with wholehearted enthusiasm. There were some that he made immortal by his generous praise. But there were others that he criticized with the sharpest severity. He called them hypocrites. He called them sons of the devil. He called them a generation of snakes. He fairly scourged them with the sword of his mouth as he wondered in the white heat of his moral indignation how they could escape the damnation of hell. As Christians we are to share his nature. We are in some measure to see through his eyes. If we do this, it may lead us at times to play the role of critic.

37

II

Since all of us criticize, how can we make our criticism Christian?

1. If we are to be Christian in our criticism, we must seek to be scrupulously honest and just. This determination I am sure would reduce our criticism to a minimum. For in order to be just we must be sure of our facts. So often we dare to criticize when we are not sure. We accept as true the flimsiest hearsay. This is dangerous. To criticize another for what that one has not done is to be at once dishonest and unjust. Sometime ago a man spoke to me in sharpest criticism of the church of which he was a part. According to him that church was on the way out. But it so happened that I was sufficiently acquainted with his church to know that his criticism had no foundation in fact. Therefore, I dared to offer the following answer: "You are making a mistake. To proclaim the failure of your church, even when it is failing, is at once bad business and bad psychology. To proclaim such failure when it is not true, is not only bad psychology, but it is dishonest." Before we can justly criticize we must be sure of our facts.

Not only must we be sure of our facts, but we must also take into consideration the background of those facts. We must know something of the causes and motives. Two men may be guilty of the same crime, and one be far less guilty than the other. We must know something of the opportunities each has had.

We must see more than the failure and the fall. We must see something of the pressure that was brought and of the fight that took place before the fall. This, of course, leads us into a realm where we cannot always walk with an assured tread. Since, therefore, we agree that if we criticize we ought to be just, and since to be just requires so much more knowledge than most of us possess, we cannot fail to realize that we ought to criticize sparingly.

2. If we are to criticize as Christians, we must do so in a spirit of good will. That is, we must seek through our criticism the highest good, both of the one criticized and of our fellows as well. Naturally this would also greatly reduce our critical output. Why do we criticize? It is not unfair to say that we are not always seeking to help. Sometimes we are doing just the opposite. Often we are angry with the one that we criticize. We are seeking to do positive hurt. We are eager to cause pain. We are thus using our tongues to fight instead of resorting to cruder weapons such as fists and guns. That harsh word that you are preparing to say, are you saying it in a spirit of good will, or in a spirit of bitterness? If you are speaking the truth in genuine love, all right. If not, you had better keep silent.

If you remind me that Jesus sometimes uttered harsh criticism, I will confess the rightness of your position. But I will remind you further that Jesus never criticized in anger. When men abused and slandered him, he did not lose his temper and answer in a spirit of revenge. "When he was reviled, he reviled not again." He used criticism as a kindly surgeon uses the knife, to cut out and cure that which he knew would destroy. In his sharp criticism of the Pharisees, for instance, he was not seeking to hurt them, but to win them from a course that he knew was working ruin. Above all else he was trying to save them in order to save the people who were following such blind guides. Therefore, to criticize aright we must be at once just and kind and brotherly.

3. Not only are we to be just and kind, but we are also to be constructive. We have agreed that by our criticism we are to seek not to hurt but to help. This in itself requires that our criticism be constructive. Nothing is more futile than to undertake to help by merely tearing down. If we pull tares and do nothing more, we may achieve a barren field. But our failure lies in the fact that by our tare-pulling we cannot guarantee a single grain of wheat. It is useless to fight any form of evil unless you have a good to put in its place. Christian criticism therefore must be not only just and kind, but constructive as well.

4. Finally, to criticize as Christians we must be at once humble and cautious. We should be humble because of the realization of our own limitations. We need to realize how little we know, not only of the facts, but especially of the hidden motives behind the facts. We need humility because it is only in such

spirit that we can have any strong hope of criticizing helpfully. "Brethren, if a man be overtaken in a fault, ye who are spiritual, restore such a one in the spirit of meekness." Why in the spirit of meekness? Because we do not take kindly to those who stand upon a pedestal to rebuke us. Such proud critics usually do far more harm than good.

Then we need humility and caution because criticism is so dangerous. To handle it carelessly is like playing with nitroglycerin. Such careless handling may work sad havoc both to the critic and to others as well. Your reputation is a part of the capital on which you do business. If one steals or tarnishes that reputation, however innocent you may be, your usefulness is impaired. But you are not the only one that is hurt thereby. They whom you might have helped also share your loss. There was once a father, a keen and capable man, devoted to his church, but he was given to the habit of criticizing his minister in the presence of his children. One day a crisis came in the life of one of his boys. In his desperation he appealed to his pastor for help. That pastor sought eagerly to comply with his request. But there was little or nothing that he could do. This was the case because the father himself had already torn that pastor's reputation to shreds.

But if criticism often endangers others, it works its deadliest harm to the critic. Years ago I knew a capable and popular physician who became a drug addict. From a highly useful man he became a worthless wreck. I have also known a few who have allowed themselves to become criticism addicts. We realize that the man who trifles with drugs plays the fool. In so trifling he may become a slave. The man who trifles with criticism is often equally foolish. For criticism, like opium or liquor, is a narcotic. It produces an appetite for itself. The more we criticize, the more we desire to criticize. Not only so, but the more we criticize, the surer we become of ourselves and the more suspicious we become of others. Here then is a dangerous weapon that we may sometimes feel ourselves called upon to wield. But we should always seek to wield it with justice and kindness, humility and caution. In no undertaking, I am persuaded, do we stand in greater need of the guidance of our Lord.

III

But if it is important that we learn to criticize aright, it is no less important that we learn how to take criticism. Often, in the language of the street, we know how to give it, but we do not know how to take it. In fact, the more critical we are, the less likely we are to take criticism in the right way. How often have I observed that those who take pride in speaking their minds to all and sundry are the ones that are likely to be most enraged when one of their fellows uses equal frankness in dealing with themselves. Here then is a very practical question. We are all at times called upon to face criticism. How shall we do it?

CRITICS AND CRITICISM

1. *There are certain wrong ways that we ought to avoid.*

(1) For instance, there are those who quit under criticism. These make their plans, set their goals, and begin work in good faith. But straightway somebody begins to criticize. Somebody tells them that what they are undertaking is foolish, or that it is impossible, or that it is not worth doing anyway. At once the hope and courage of the one criticized drops to zero. "Maybe you are right," is the spineless answer. Then the tools fall from his nerveless hands and he gives over his dreams. Such poor souls are like the wheat that was sown upon stony ground. They may flourish for a little while, but under the hot sun of criticism they wither and die.

(2) Then there are those that surrender in another fashion. These listen to every critic that comes their way. They also assume that what the critic says is always right. This unfortunate chap tries to take everybody's advice. If two or more bands are playing, he seeks to keep step with them all. I knew a minister like this not many years ago. He was suddenly promoted to a large church. He was so eager to hold his position that he listened to all who sought to advise him. I think I have never known a man more eager to please. But in his eagerness to please everybody he ended in pleasing nobody, not even himself.

(3) Then there are those who take the opposite course. Instead of listening to everybody, they listen

to nobody. Every suggestion is an affront, every criticism an insult. The more these are criticized, the more stubborn and set in their ways they become. They never seek for the truth that might be in the criticism. They are too busy looking for the stupidity, envy, and ill will that they are sure are lurking in the heart of the critic. By and by these reach the place where their best friends will not tell them anything. They will not dare, because they know that to do so would be to get themselves hated, and that for nothing.

2. *But there are some right ways to meet criticism.*

(1) Some criticism we ought to ignore. Suppose, for instance, one criticizes you out of sheer malice. For you to grow hot and resentful is only to play into your critic's hands. Surely the best way to answer such criticism is to ignore it. Suppose, on the other hand, your critic is honest but ill informed as to your business as well as to yourself. For instance, if Fritz Kreisler were to give a concert in our city tomorrow night and I should come out the following morning with a sharp criticism, then what? I have an idea that this great artist would first ask what I know about music in general, and the violin in particular. I have an idea, further, that when he found that all my musical knowledge amounted to just even nothing, he would simply ignore what I had to say. Criticism born of ill will or of ignorance, as a rule, should not be noticed.

(2) Some criticisms we should use. Sometimes our critics speak the truth. Sometimes we can find them

really helpful. Years ago I was sent to be pastor of a prominent college church. I was very timid, and my first service filled me with terror. I managed to get through somehow because the Lord was merciful and the congregation on the whole very kind. But there was one heartless wretch who, instead of praising my sermon, told how many times I had scratched the left side of my head with my right hand. The number was distressingly large, certainly out of all proportion to the way my head was itching. Frankly, I did not enjoy his criticism in the least. But I did not grow red in the face and affirm that he was not telling the truth. Instead, I determined then and there to reduce my public scratching to the lowest terms. Regardless of my lack of appreciation, my critic helped me in this instance, just as others have done again and again.

Then our critics can often help us in the doing of our work. They give us a large part of all the free advertising that we get. Sometimes, even when hostile, they are almost as useful as friends. For instance, we owe an immeasurable debt to those friends of Jesus who have given us such priceless insights into his teaching and character. But the critics of our Lord have also made a contribution of surpassing value. It was a critic that put his finger on a fundamental fact in the life of Jesus by saying, "He trusted in God." It was a critic that said, "He saved others, himself he cannot save," thus making vivid a truth that Jesus had constantly taught by what he was and by what he said and did. It was a critic that gave hope to the hopeless and despised by calling the Master a friend of publicans and sinners. There are some criticisms, therefore, that we ought to use.

(3) Finally, some criticism we ought to defy and contradict. A few centuries ago a queer chap got it into his head that the earth was round. Those who heard his wild theory called him a crack-brain and a fool. But this man, instead of going into a rage, defied their criticism by proving the truthfulness of his contention. When the Wright brothers first began trying to make an airship, one critic declared boldly that no airship would ever be invented. He even went further and affirmed that if one were invented it would not be by the Wright brothers. What did these brave workers have to say to that? They defied and contradicted him by persisting in their work till their mad dream had become a reality. And Jesus, crucified as an impostor, contradicted his murderers by passing through Black Friday to Easter morning.

Here then is a message that we all need. I am sure that it is needed by the pastor as genuinely as it is by you who sit in the pew. We all dare at times the delicate and dangerous role of critic. Let us see to it that we bring our criticism into harmony with the mind of Christ. That means that we shall only criticize when we can do so with justice, with kindness, with humility, and constructively. To criticize in any other fashion is to hurt both ourselves and others. Let us seek also to face criticism in the same spirit that our Lord faced the criticism that came to him. If we do this, we shall refuse to quit under criticism. We shall refuse to accept all criticism, or bitterly and stubbornly to reject all. Some of it we shall ignore, some we shall use, some we shall defy. By so doing we shall find even criticism one of those "all things" that work together by the grace of God for our good.

IV

THE LITTLE OUTLAW

"And one of the malefactors which were hanged railed on him, saying, If thou be the Christ, save thyself and us."

LUKE 23:39

I

JESUS, AS YOU KNOW, DIED BETWEEN TWO OUTLAWS. These outlaws had been companions in crime. They had pillaged and shed blood together. So far as we know, they had been arrested at the same time. Together they had stood trial. Together they had been condemned. Together they had walked to the place of execution, each bearing his own cross. Together they are now dying. On the surface there seems little to choose between them. Yet, in my opinion, they are as far apart as the spaces between the stars. One of these outlaws has a bigness about him that thrills us to this day. But the impression made by his companion is that of littleness. He strikes me as a man whose pettiness is even more pronounced than his wickedness.

Of course, when we speak of bigness and littleness we are referring to moral qualities. To determine the size of a man we do not put the measuring string either around his body or around his mind, we put it around his heart. For this reason we realize that one might be mediocre in his mental capacity, small in his achievements, yet great in his soul. For instance, when I think of one of the truly great men it has been my privilege to know, I think of an ex-slave, Uncle Jesse by name, who used to live on my father's farm. Uncle Jesse could neither read nor write. His material wealth would not have brought a thousand dollars in any market. But I never knew him to do a mean or petty deed. He had the courage of which heroes are made. He had a loyalty that was beautiful, deep, and abiding. Therefore, I think of Uncle Jesse as one of the big men that I have known.

On the other hand there are those that are big in ability and big in achievement, but petty in soul. It is said that a certain multimillionaire when asked for a donation for a good cause, took a coin from his pocket, looked at it, then put it back, saying, "I could spare the principal, but could not spare the interest." He was a great financier, but a little man. A few years ago I read a brilliantly written piece of fiction that was marred by deliberate filthiness. It was a bit like rotten mackerel in the moonlight. It glittered while it smelled to high heaven. The author was a gifted writer, but a cheap man. There is no doubt that history will have to give to Hitler a place as one of the supreme military geniuses of all time. But, though a great warrior, he is a little man. With the military ability of a giant, he has the soul of a pygmy. How talented this outlaw was we cannot say. But of this I feel sure, that he was a little man.

II

What right have we to bring against him this ugly accusation? We get only one view of his face. He comes upon the stage only one time. He utters only one brief sentence. These may seem very small data upon which to pass judgment. But the scientist does not need a whole bay to tell the nature of the water of the ocean; he needs only one drop. He does not need a whole skeleton to tell what the animal looked like in life; he needs only one bone. Just so we do not need the whole panorama of a man's life to form some opinion of the kind of man he was. Often one view is enough. This one scene on Calvary is a window through which we can look into this man's soul. What we see when we thus look are marks of extreme littleness.

1. This outlaw was little in that he permitted himself to mouth criticisms, insults, and slanders without any regard to the facts in the case. The chances are

that this man had never seen Jesus before. He therefore knew very little about him. Yet, when the religious leaders and the mob began to pelt him with insults, without any regard to the merits of the case, without any effort to find out the truth, he joined his voice with theirs. Such conduct is ever a mark of littleness. To take up any sort of a position against an individual or an institution without giving yourself a chance to investigate and know the facts is not a mark of bigness but of pettiness. Just what caused this outlaw to join the enemies of Jesus we are not told. He probably did so for one or more of these petty reasons.

First, he may have been a mere imitator. Hearing this pack of human hounds yelping at Jesus, he may have joined in just to be with the crowd. He may have been a worshiper of the god of numbers. He may have bowed at the shrine of noise. There are always those that do this. They take their positions without any regard to the right and wrong of the matter. They have an eye only for the conduct of the crowd. Therefore, when asked for their reason for doing anything, good or bad, they have no better answer than, "Everybody was doing it." These never dare to dress their lives by their own mirrors. They always dress by the mirror that is held up by the hand of the crowd.

At their best such people are merely weak and silly. At their worst they may become positively criminal.

Some years ago I saw a cartoon that pictures such petty souls. A woman was riding down a country path on a bicycle. At a spot where this path was bisected at a right angle by a second path, this lady encountered a flock of sheep. But the leader of that flock was not only a polite sheep, but also an athletic one. Therefore, he leaped over the woman, bicycle and all, and thus permitted her to ride on in safety. But the second sheep came and leaped high into the air just as his leader. Thus also did the third, and the fourth. In fact the whole big flock leaped one by one, though by the time they had finished the woman was at home in bed. Had you asked this last sheep for the cause of his leaping, you know what he would have answered? Just this: "Everybody jumped." But such conduct is little, whether it characterizes a sheep or a man.

Then, this outlaw might have joined in the hue and cry against Jesus because of prejudice. Rumors about this Man had been blown about the country for many months. Possible this robber had heard these rumors, and without trying to find out whether they were true or not, had become prejudiced. Or he may have been prejudiced against Jesus because he was a rabbi and he did not like rabbis. There is no accounting for his prejudice any more than for ours. We often dislike folks for no better reason than that they belong to some other church, or to some other race, or to some other nation. Prejudice is a blindfold by which we often bandage our eyes. It is a kind of wool that we stuff into our ears that enables us to hear the bad, but makes us deaf to the good. While this greater outlaw so saw and heard that he was remade, this little outlaw, blinded and deafened by his prejudice, saw nothing except something to make him howl and sneer.

Possibly this petty outlaw may have railed upon Jesus for an even meaner reason. When the work of crucifixion was over, and the Master was hanging on the cross, he prayed this amazing prayer: "Father, forgive them; for they know not what they do." Both these robbers saw the dying Man and heard his prayer, but with what different results! When the great robber saw and heard, it broke his heart. Against the white background of this fine Soul, he came to see his own moral ugliness. Thus seeing, though he was even now suffering the very pangs of hell, he declared that he was suffering justly. But while this little robber heard the same prayer and looked into the same face, he saw nothing that gave him either humility or hope. He was not softened in the least, but made only the more hard and bitter and angry. What was the matter? It would seem that this greatness that he could not quite keep from recognizing in Jesus served only to fill him with the poison of resentment.

Was this little outlaw then envious of Jesus? It would seem so. It is hard to explain his hate in any other way. Envy, as you know, is ever a child of hate. "Love envieth not." Not only is it a child of

53

hate, but it is a child of hate at its meanest. The envious man does not seek to climb up to his victorious brother, he seeks rather to drag him down and thrust him below himself. When the Younger Son came home and a feast was made in his honor, the Elder Son would not go in. The honor being shown his repentant brother filled him with envy. He was so envious that he sought to spoil the feast for others as well as for himself. Envy is as deadly as it is ugly. It was born with a murderer's club in its hand, and has been in the bloody business ever since. Yet, there are few of us that have not at times been little enough to give way to this ugly child of hate. This outlaw, then, might have insulted the Master because he was an imitator, or because he was prejudiced, or because His greatness filled him with envy and hate. But whatever the reason, his conduct seems that of a petty soul.

2. Then the pettiness of this man is further seen when we hear him pray. The words of our text are a kind of prayer. Through them we get a glimpse of this man in his closet. There is no better way to tell the caliber of a man than to hear him pray. Here, for instance, are some Christians upon their knees. They have come upon times of peril. Their backs are to the wall, persecution is abroad, and there is likely to be some blood-letting. For what do they pray under these trying circumstances? Listen. "And now, Lord, behold there are threatenings." Then what? They do not

pray for escape, they do not pray for an easy time. "And now, Lord, behold their threatenings; and grant unto thy servants, that with all boldness they may speak thy word." They pray that, whatever comes, they may see it through without shame to themselves and without dishonor to their Lord. That prayer marks them as great in soul.

But the prayer of this little outlaw is petty like himself. Listen: "If thou be the Christ, save thyself and us." First, it is petty in its extent. For whom does he pray? At most for himself and for his companion. But as we read between the lines, I think we may be sure that he is concerned only about himself. Now, to pray for one's self is at times altogether right. When the Publican said, "God be merciful unto me a sinner," he was praying a big prayer. But the tragedy is that often our prayers begin and end there. We only have a hat-wide view of human need. We are concerned solely about ourselves. But if we are Christian our view must be broader. We may begin in a small way. We may be interested only in ourselves and those that come closest to us; but if we are Christlike, we must broaden till we have a map of the world upon our hearts.

Then if his prayer was petty in extent it was even more petty in its content. But you answer, "Was he not praying for salvation?" Indeed he was! But what a small word salvation was upon his lips. Salvation rightly understood is the biggest something for which we can pray. There is nothing that the individual, that society, that the world needs today so much as salvation. It is to save his people that Jesus has come. But what is the salvation he offers? It is a salvation that means forgiveness of sin. It means the restoration of the broken friendship between man and God. It means life abundant. It means that sharing in the divine nature that sends us out to live Christlike lives. But what did salvation mean on the lips of this little outlaw? It only meant escape. He was saying to Jesus: "Take me down from the cross. I do not mind being a sinner, but I do not wish to suffer for my sin. I do not mind being what I am, but I hate to be where I am. I have no objections to being a crook, but I am eager to enjoy my crookedness. I am not the least concerned about the character, but I am greatly concerned about comfort."

What a petty prayer! Yet, let him that is without the same sin cast the first stone at this robber. It strikes me that this is one of the most prevalent prayers of our day. There are multitudes that seem to feel that all that is necessary to bring in the Kingdom is for everybody to draw a pension, ride on a pass, and live without working. General Petain points out the fact that this love of ease on the part of France was one of the great causes of her downfall. Such a conception of salvation is a menace always, both to the individual and to the nation. Easy Street may be comfortable, but too often it ends in Rotten Road. Surely one of the major dangers that threaten us today is the widespread clamor for an easy patriotism, an easy church life, an easy religion. It would seem that the ambition and prayers of multitudes might be summed up in this childish word:

"I wish I was president of these United States,
I'd eat molasses candy and swing upon the gates."

III

What did his littleness do for this outlaw?

1. It tortured him. Crucifixion was agony enough, but he added to his agony by allowing himself to be so little. Pettiness is often the mother of pain. How much we suffer, not because our fellows are deliberately cruel and unkind, but because we take a little and mean view of things. There are those who cannot hear of the good fortune of a friend without a pang. There are those who actually go out in search of insults. There are those who can find cruelty where only kindness was intended. I knew a mother once who became unspeakably bitter because her daughters did not receive as much attention from our church as she thought they ought to receive. She accused us of neglecting them because they were poor. When this attention was increased she was equally bitter. She declared that we helped only to emphasize her poverty. Thus when treated with no conspicuous kindness she felt herself neglected. When shown kindness beyond the ordi-

57

nary, she felt herself insulted. Truly littleness is a burden grievous to be borne.

2. Then to be little is to hurt others. We have read much about the nuisance vaiue of Italy to Germany. Littleness has a great nuisance value for the powers of evil. One reason the flea is such a pest is because he is so small. It is bad to be swallowed by a whale, but to be nibbled to death by minnows is more painful still. How many homes are wrecked by sheer pettiness on the part of husband or wife, or both! After listening to stories of domestic tragedy for more than a quarter of a century, I have reached the conclusion that it is not the big things as a rule that wreck marriage, but the little things. It is the little foxes that spoil the marital vine. Multitudes that can weather heavy storms on the high seas often make shipwreck in a bathtub. In fact, one of the deadliest foes to home, church, and state is littleness. This robber, therefore, by allowing himself to be little, became a torture to himself and a burden and hindrance to his fellows.

3. Finally, this man's littleness caused him to miss the biggest and finest opportunity of his life. Small as he was, there was offered him a chance in this trying hour of crucifixion to become great. His companion in crime took that chance. Being big enough to see through his own eyes, this man saw in Jesus that which made him ashamed and penitent while it gave him hope. Therefore, he prayed this winsome prayer, "Jesus, remember me when thou comest into thy king-

dom." And Jesus answered, "Today shalt thou be with me in paradise." But what did he answer this petty robber? Nothing at all. There are prayers that are so little and mean that God cannot answer them. This little outlaw might have gone out into the land of eternal progress in the fellowship of Jesus, had he not allowed his pettiness to make him blind.

IV

But is there a cure for littleness? Are not some born little while others are born great? Of course, some are naturally greater than others. But since the littleness of which we speak is a moral quality, nobody is born petty. We only make ourselves so by our mean and petty choices. Do you remember the magic vest that when put on made every wish of the wearer come true? But there was this difficulty: Every time the wearer made a selfish wish the vest drew up a bit and thus made the wearer a smaller man. Therefore, since we become small from choice, we can also take the path to greatness from choice. How shall we become victors over our littleness?

1. Face the sin and ugliness of it, and make a determined fight against it. It is well to begin every day with this prayer: "Lord, I am going out into a world that will try me. I may be disappointed. I may be insulted. I may have my opinions set aside. I may have to see others take the position that I desired and to which I felt myself entitled. I may have to see

my rival elected, while I go down in defeat. I may have to see my friend make a touchdown, while I fumble the ball. Whatever happens, save me from littleness. Help me to meet whatever comes, whether victory or defeat, with bigness of soul."

2. Not only must we pray and fight against littleness, but we must fight positively. The only way to drive darkness out of a room is to bring in the light. The one foe of littleness is bigness. Henry Ward Beecher was a great preacher. But nothing finer was said about him than this: "Whoever did him an injury could count with assurance upon having that injury repaid by kindness." Booker T. Washington was a kindred spirit. Hear him as he says, "I resolved that I would permit no man to narrow and degrade my soul by making me hate him." Lincoln possessed this type of bigness to a superlative degree. When Stanton called him "the original gorilla," he retaliated by putting him into his cabinet. The supreme foe of littleness is bigness.

3. Finally, let God into your life. Here is a fact upon which we may count with perfect confidence: our God can make little souls into big souls. What a small man was John when he first met Jesus! He was so little that he was eager to call down fire from heaven upon certain ignorant villagers that had refused him and his Master a night's lodging. Yet, how big he became in the fellowship of Christ! He became so great that he could take the whole world to his

heart.   This same Christ is eager for us to set our feet upon the path to largeness of heart.   "Beloved, now are we the sons of God, and it doth yet appear what we shall be: but we know that, when he shall appear, we shall be like him; for we shall see him as he is." All of us, therefore, have in us the capacity for greatness of soul.   This is the gospel that it is my privilege to bring to you at this hour.

V

THE GREAT OUTLAW

"Jesus, remember me when thou comest into thy kingdom."

LUKE 23:42

❈

THE MAN WHO PRAYED THIS PRAYER IS WELL worth knowing. It strikes me that he was possessed of genuine greatness. In fact, of all the faces that we see about the cross, his, I think, is the most striking and inspiring. How this big soul came to be what he is and where he is we can only guess. Of this we may be sure, he never set out with Calvary as his goal. In his youth, I dare say, he was the most enthusiastic and ardent of patriots. He had resolved to live for only one high purpose: to free his people from the yoke of Rome. Of course, he knew that there were great risks to be run. But with a fine high courage he dedicated himself to the task of winning freedom both for his fellows and for himself. Little did he dream that all his fine hopes would end like this. Little did he think when he set out on youth's bright morning that his story would be punctuated at last by a grim period in the form of a cross.

But if his goal was far different from what he had expected, what he had become before reaching that goal was still less expected. At first I am confident this man had sought to gain his ends by legitimate means. But he had been disappointed by both his friends and his foes. Little by little, therefore, he came to despair of gaining his ends within the law. More and more he began to put his confidence in violence. Being unable to organize an army and to fight in the open, he organized a guerrilla band that hovered in the fastnesses of the mountains and swooped down to attack small detachments of Roman soldiers. Then, under pressure, he had ceased to confine himself to the Romans. He and his men degenerated into a clan of robbers. One day their victims made resistance; then blood-letting became a necessity. He recoiled from this at first, but by and by he became hardened. Thus, if one had told him in the days of his youth that he would end on a cross he would have been surprised. But if one had told him that before he reached the cross he would have already crucified his better self he would have been more surprised still. But here he is dying on Calvary, not as a clean and ardent patriot, but as a disgraced and hardened criminal.

But there was something else that happened that day that, had he been forewarned, would have surprised him most of all. Suppose a friend had said to him as he began his march down the Via Dolorosa, "Before the day is over you will be praying to this Prisoner who is so weak from loss of blood that even now he is staggering under the weight of his cross." Do you suppose this outlaw would have believed it? By no means. Such a prophecy he would doubtless have answered with sarcasm, if not with oaths. "I pray? I have given up that foolishness long ago. I do not even pray to God any more. But if I were going to pray I certainly would not pray to a man who is weaker than myself. I would not pray to one who is silly enough to go out in the spirit of a lamb to fight with a multitude of lions." Yet, a few hours later this bold, hard man is sobbing out this prayer: "Jesus, remember me when thou comest into thy kingdom."

I

How did this great outlaw come thus to pray?

1. He really saw Jesus. It was the marvelous insight of the man that led to his praying and to his transformation. When we consider the circumstance it seems impossible to exaggerate the fine insight of this great soul. There was everything humanly speaking to obscure his vision. The religious leaders of the

day, the men of light and learning, were taunting this man on the central cross. They could find no words too bitter to say to him. The crowd, under their influence, was mouthing their denunciations with them. The hard Roman soldiers joined their voices to that of the crowd just to be with the majority. Then this robber and his companion under the spell of the mob-mind joined their jibes with the others. There was a bedlam of shrieks, every one of which was an insult.

But something happened to this outlaw that struck him dumb. The taunts that he was on the point of uttering died upon his lips. This man at his side is praying. He can see his lips move. Now he can hear the words of his prayer. For what is he praying? He is not praying for himself. That was amazing. He is not praying vengeance upon his enemies. He is not asking that Rome be cursed with utter ruin. That would have been this outlaw's prayer if he had prayed at all. Instead, he is saying, "Father, forgive them, for they know not what they do." He is actually finding excuses for those who are putting him to death. He is actually praying for those who are hating him and torturing him. How incredible! What a strange man! He has never met anybody like this before.

In an effort to get a better view of this amazing Man he turns as far as possible toward that middle cross. Then he sees something that he has not noticed before. It is the placard above the head of this Man of prayer. That placard bore the accusation for which Jesus was being done to death. It was also Pilate's bitter insult to his enemies. It was his way of plaguing and taunting these people whom he has come to hate and despise. The placard reads like this: "Jesus, the King of the Jews." That was not only the insult, but the joke of the day. Those who read it laughed scornfully, if they were able to forget the insult that it contained. How ridiculous to call this dying Man a king!

Once that was the view of this great outlaw, but it is not so any more. He alone has read this inscription aright. This man is a king, he is the King. The reality of his kingship breaks upon him with irresistible conviction. True his only throne is a cross, his only crown is one of thorns, his only scepter the nails that pin his hands. His whole royal wardrobe is in the hands of the Roman crap-shooters. Yet this man of marvelous insight looks past all these hindrances and sees Jesus for what he is, the King.

Not only does he see him as a King, but as a spotless King. Rome has declared Jesus guilty of high treason. The religious leaders of the day have pronounced him a blasphemer and an impostor, but this daring outlaw reverses both these sentences. "This man," he says, "has done nothing amiss." What insight and courage it took to say this! He is going to speak for himself a little later, but before he speaks for himself he speaks for this dying man at his side. He sees in him

66

a King who is spotless, perfect in purity, perfect in his holiness. It was this clear insight that was the first step toward transformation.

2. Seeing Jesus, he came to see himself. When this outlaw was first arrested, when he was nailed upon his cross, I feel confident that he had no regrets for the wrongs that he had done. His one regret was that he had not been able to do more. Rome had pronounced him guilty, but he did not agree with that hard sentence. But he does now. Against the white background of the Man at his side he has seen himself. Thus seeing himself he declares, "We receive the due reward of our deeds." He is suffering the very pangs of hell, but he says that it is no more than he deserves. We complain today of our lost sensitiveness toward sin. Most of us are not worried in the least about our little sins. Even when we confess them our confessions lack reality. They do not burst from us red with shame and wet with tears. Why is this the case? It is because we compare ourselves with ourselves. It is because of a lost sense of God. We do not see ourselves in the light of his holiness.

This robber might have died a hard and self-satisfied criminal. This he certainly would have done if he had looked only at his fellows. "I am dying as a criminal," he might have said, "but I am no worse than this companion of mine, who is also dying for his crime. I am an outlaw, it is true; but in spite of that I am a saint in comparison with white-haired old

Annas, who has grown fat on cruelty and oppression." But when he looked into the face of Jesus, he had no good word to say for himself. He could only declare that even in crucifixion he was suffering no more than he deserved. That is ever the case with those who really see God. Young Isaiah was doubtless one of the cleanest men of his day. Yet, when he saw the Lord he could only sob out this confession: "I am a man of unclean lips." In the light of the divine countenance we get a vision of our own hearts and know ourselves for what we are, and that is as sinners.

3. Not only did this outlaw see himself when he saw Jesus, but he also realized something of his possibilities. If Jesus convicts us of our sin, he also convicts us of the possibilities of salvation. He makes us hope. He makes us see the dawning of a better tomorrow. This outlaw knows himself a sinner. The guilt that tortures his soul is so intense that he has almost forgotten the pangs of crucifixion. But he dimly sees a way of escape. This dying Man at his side can help him. Therefore, he changes that cross, with its howls of derision, into a closet where he makes his prayer. If Jesus has driven him to despair, he has also kindled in his soul an amazing hope beyond all his dreams.

II

Notice next the prayer of this outlaw. It is just such a prayer as we should expect from a great soul.

1. To whom does he pray? The answer to that question may astonish some of us. He does not pray to God the Father. He does not begin as Jesus teaches us to begin by saying, "Our Father, who are in heaven." He rather prays to Jesus himself. Think of the daring of a faith like that. This outlaw is dying and he knows it. This Man at his side is dying more rapidly than himself. He knows that too. Yet, this dying robber turns to this shamed, defeated, and dying Christ and makes to him his prayer. How that must have heartened Jesus! How our Lord must have appreciated it! The multitude was howling insults, but only one man so far as we know in all the world was honoring this dying King by praying to him. And that man was an outlaw, whose face he had perhaps never seen before they went out to die together.

2. For whom does this outlaw pray? He does not pray for the wide world. He does not pray for his needy nation. He does not pray for his companion in crime. He prays for himself. Prayer for others is at once a high privilege and duty. To refuse to pray for others is to refuse to live up to the best. "God forbid that I should sin against the Lord in ceasing to pray for you." We appreciate this unselfish sentiment:

> "Help me to live from day to day
> In such a self-forgetful way,
> That, even when I kneel to pray,
>   My prayer shall be for others."

But there are times when we are hardly fit to pray for others. There are times when the connection between us and God is broken down. Before we talk to the King about others, we must win our way into his presence. The door by which we thus enter is a prayer that is intensely personal. "Have mercy upon me, O God," prays the penitent Psalmist. "God be merciful to me," said the publican who went down to his house justified. "Lord, remember me," prays this robber. For him, there are only two beings in the universe at this moment—Jesus and himself.

3. For what does he pray? Here again we see the marks of his true greatness. He does not ask Jesus to save him from the consequences of his sin. He does not ask of this dying Man that he take him down from the cross. His hell is not in being where he is, it is in being what he is. Not only does he not ask for escape, he does not ask for position or power. The ambitious sons of Zebedee, praying about the coming Kingdom, sought a place, the one on the right and the other on the left. But not so with this great outlaw. He does not give Jesus a blue print of all his needs. He makes one inclusive request: "Jesus, remember me when thou comest into thy kingdom."

"In spite of all appearances," he seems to say, "you are King. Since you are King, this is not the end for you. I know that this cross is utterly powerless to destroy you. It does not put a period to your life. It is not even a comma. You are going to be done with

70

it in a moment. Soon the storm will be over and you will be experiencing the eternal calm. Soon you will have passed from bleak winter into an abiding spring. Soon you will have passed through this black tunnel out under the blue skies of God's eternal morning. When you have done this, remember the outlaw at whose side you died." Notice his firm confidence. "Jesus, remember me," he prays, not "if thou comest." There is no *if* about it. But, "remember me when thou comest." He feels that this Man is sure to win, and that, having won, a single thought on his part will suffice him for time and eternity. No faith could be greater than that.

III

What response did Jesus make to this daring prayer? This outlaw had prayed to him as a King. As a King Jesus made his response. He gave to this man a royal word. He did not tell this poor robber, "You have put more weight upon me than I can bear." With superb majesty he answered: "Today shalt thou be with me in Paradise." What a rich and satisfying answer! Look at something of its wealth.

1. It blots out the period that some think death puts to life. "Thou shalt be," says Jesus with quiet assurance. "Since you have asked that I remember you beyond the cross, you assume that I am going to continue to live. You are right in so assuming. I am the resurrection and the life. Death cannot stop me.

No more can it stop you. Because I live, you shall live also. This is not the end, it is only a glorious beginning. Verily I say unto thee, Today shalt thou be with me in Paradise."

2. Not only does he promise this dying robber a future life, but he promises him a life in fellowship with himself. "Thou shalt be with me." "You are with me here," he seems to say. "Here in this strange ordeal we have met and joined hands and hearts. Because we have thus met, nothing can separate us. I have found you. I love you too well ever to let you go. Today and tomorrow and forever thou shalt be with me. The place of meeting is to be Paradise, but it is not Paradise that makes the meeting worth while, it is the fellowship with me."

3. This beautiful consummation was not to take place in some far-off tomorrow. When are these two who are rapidly slipping from life to find each other again? "At the resurrection of the last day," you answer. "Thousands of years hence, perhaps millions, then maybe they will meet." So many believe, though such is not the faith of the New Testament. Kipling says we shall "lie down for an æon or two." How many æons were Jesus and this outlaw to lie down? Not for one æon, not for one instant. Together they went away; together they appeared an instant later in the presence of God. The robber, as his Master, was possessed of a quality of life over which death had no power.

Here then is a gospel for this hour. It is a gospel
for you and for me. If this outlaw, in spite of all his
hindrances, could find life eternal, surely we ought not
to despair. The road that he took that brought him
courage to face death and eternity unafraid we also
may take. It is one that bears the footmarks of all
the saints. We must begin where the robber began,
with the fact of our sin. We must turn to Jesus as he
did for help and healing. In doing this, we too shall
find life. We shall find it in the here and now. We
shall find it instantly. And finding life here, it will
be our portion to the end of the journey, and through
the journey, and until we awake in his likeness on the
other side.

T OUTLAW

eternal, surely we ought not
that he took that brought him
and straightway afraid we also
that bears the footmarks of all
begin where the robber began.

and faith here and now. We
And during life here, it will
the end of the journey, and through
until we awake in his likeness on the

VI

THE CONSCRIPT

"And they compel one Simon a Cyrenian, who passed by, coming out of the country, the father of Alexander and Rufus, to bear his cross."

MARK 15:21

JESUS HAS BEEN SENTENCED TO DEATH. IN COMpany with two rugged outlaws he is making his way to that skull-shaped hill called Calvary. Each of the condemned men is bearing his own cross. About the same time that this procession of death was beginning its march from the palace of Herod, a certain man, Simon by name, was setting out from the house of a friend, headed toward Jerusalem. This man has come all the way from Africa to attend the feast. Possibly this is his first visit to the city of his fathers. He is all eagerness and enthusiasm. Having spent the

74

night in the country on account of the crowded condition of the city, he is now making his way back to its busy streets to thrill at the sights that it has to offer.

As he reaches the city gate he encounters a crowd that is going in the opposite direction. This multitude excites his curiosity. Though he is the father of a family, he is still little more than a big, overgrown boy. He is possessed of a thoroughly normal curiosity. He inquires of one of the crowd as to what is going on. "We are going to Calvary," comes the answer, "to execute three prisoners." Simon's curiosity is greatly heightened by this word. He has never been present at an execution. This is his chance. At least he will see the men who are doomed to die. Therefore, being a bold and husky chap, he elbows his way through the crowd till he obtains what amounts to a ringside seat.

There go the three doomed men, each bearing his own cross. They are so close that he could almost touch them with his hand. Those two in front march steadily forward. They are lithe and sinewy and strong as steel. Their tanned faces are bold and hard. With the crowd they exchange jibe for jibe. Like men they have fought, like men they are determined to die. Simon gives them a grudging admiration. Since they have earned the death penalty, he is glad they are going to see it through without whining. But the other Prisoner is vastly different. His face is not hard at all. It is full of an infinite pity, mingled with immeasurable sorrow and pain. Then, too, though a man of fine physique, he is not up to the task of bearing his own cross. He has lost too much blood. In fact, while Simon is looking, this Prisoner staggers and falls, his cross crushing him to the ground.

Simon is a bit sorry; he wishes that this weaker Prisoner could see it through in a more manly fashion. But of course there is nothing that he can do about it. Having satisfied his curiosity, he is on the point of losing himself in the crowd or continuing his journey into the city. But just as he is turning away a heavy hand grips his shoulder, and a voice, harsh and authoritative startles him. "You, there, make yourself useful! Take up that cross and get going!" Simon cannot believe that he has heard aright. Surely this soldier is not talking to him. Surely not even a Roman dog would tell a man, who was convicted of no offense, to take up a cross and bear it, as if he were a criminal sentenced to death. But when he starts to turn away as if he has not heard, the soldier's hand looses him and leaps to the sword at his side. Simon, seeing that he must obey, takes up the hated cross, and turns his steps toward Calvary.

Now there is a sense in which this experience of Simon's is altogether unique. No other man in all the centuries ever journeyed from the country to Jerusalem to see and do just what he did. No other man ever met this procession at the gate as did Simon.

No other man ever carried upon his shoulders the actual wooden cross upon which our Lord was crucified. This shameful ordeal gave to Simon a marvelous story to tell that is absolutely unique. But while there is that about this story that is unique, there is also that about it that makes it common to countless thousands. In this experience of Simon's we can, therefore, read not only his story, but that of many others as well.

I

The first fact about Simon's experience that makes it thoroughly human is this: One day when he was going his own carefree way, one day when his broad shoulders were carrying no burden save that of his own choosing, something happened to change all this. Suddenly, like a bolt from the blue, he found all his plans knocked to pieces. He found himself going in a direction that he would never have taken except under compulsion. He was being compelled to carry a burden that was altogether hateful. Life often does such things to us. Some of us know exactly how to sympathize with Simon. There are those, of course, who are following the road today that they chose in the long ago. But with many this is not the case. We are not doing what we once thought we would do. We are not going in the direction that we once thought we would travel. Something has happened that has compelled us utterly to change our plans.

Here, for instance, is a young chap leaving his

father's tent to visit his brothers down at Dothan. This brilliant youth is full of high hopes and dreams. He feels that he knows exactly what he is going to do with his life. He is going to become the head of his clan. He is going to become a sheik of the first order. But when his harsh and cruel brothers see him coming, they form different plans. "There comes that dreamer," they say in bitter hate. They at once decide "to feed fat the ancient grudge" they have against him. Therefore, when he arrives they tear from him his sporty coat and pitch him into an old well.

By and by some merchants come on the scene, headed toward Egypt. Then one of these brothers, who has an eye for business, makes a wise suggestion. "Let us not kill our brother," he urges with a fine show of compassion, "lest his blood be upon our hands. Instead, let us sell him, then we shall not only be guiltless of his blood, but we shall be twenty dollars to the good." "All right," they agree. Since business is business they feel that such an opportunity must not be passed up. Therefore, they sell Joseph into slavery. Thus they tear all his plans into shreds. Instead of turning his step back to his father's tent, he heads toward a slave's pen and toward a dungeon. He heads also toward a palace on the Nile. But this latter comes not of necessity, but of his living within the will of God. Thus life did for Joseph somewhat as it did for Simon.

A friend told me this story: A few years ago there was a well-to-do young farmer who was converted and felt himself called into the ministry. At once he made ready to go away to college to prepare himself for his work. To this end he began at once to convert his houses and lands and livestock into money. When everything was ready and he was being driven to the station on his way to college, something happened that upset all his plans. The team ran away, the buggy was wrecked, and his back was broken. Then followed long months of agony in a hospital. His wounds refused to heal and everything seemed to go wrong. When he was at last able to leave the hospital he was not only penniless, but a hopeless cripple. All his plans had to be given up, and his fine dreams seemed to end in nothing better than disappointment and tragedy. He kept his faith in God, but it was not easy with his whole life thus falling in ruins about him.

Not only did Simon have his plans changed, not only was he compelled to go in a different direction from that of his own choosing, but he was compelled to bear a burden not his own. He was quite sure that this heavy load that had just crushed Jesus to the ground was none of his affair. Of his own choice he would never have thought of taking such a shameful weight upon his shoulders. But he had no choice in the matter. He was compelled, this story tells us. Being thus compelled, of course, this heavy load was just a tormenting burden and nothing more. By and by, as we shall see, it was transformed into a cross. But this was the case only because he came to bear willingly what he had once borne not of choice, but from compulsion.

This also is a very human experience. Some years ago in a southern village there was a lovely young girl who was the center of her social circle. She was at once beautiful and charming. She was engaged to be married to a young chap who stood high in the community. But tragedy came into her home. Her mother and her brilliant and gifted brother died within a week of each other. Her only other brother was an imbecile. In the face of this tragedy her father lost his health and became a hopeless invalid. In order to carry the heavy load of looking after this invalid father and imbecile brother this brave girl had to give up the privilege of marriage. Then the slow years crept by and these two passed "to where beyond these voices there is peace." But by that time spring had changed to autumn, and this fresh young girl had become a white-haired old maid. Thus life often wrecks our plans and puts upon our shoulders burdens not our own.

II

What was Simon's reaction to this forbidding experience?

That is an important question. In fact, it is a question of supreme importance. It is not what life does to us that really matters, it is our reaction to what life does. By a wrong reaction we can change our wealth into want. We can change our strength into weakness, and our blessings into that which brings a curse. Many are doing just that. I have in mind a friend who, when he was a poor and struggling worker, was one of the choicest of men. But now, having succeeded beyond his dreams, he has allowed his wealth to clip the thews of his moral and spiritual strength.

But, if by a wrong reaction we can change our wealth into want, by a right reaction we can change our want into wealth. If by a wrong reaction we can make our capital into a calamity, by a right reaction we can make our calamity into unfailing capital. "To them that love God," declares Paul, speaking out of his own experience, "all things work together for good." This is true of the joy things and the sorrow things, the things that make for laughter and the things that make for tears. Paul, meeting all life's experiences within the will of God, made them to minister to his growth in grace and to his larger usefulness whether they were pleasant or unpleasant, sweet or bitter.

How then, I repeat, did Simon react to his unwelcome experience? At first I am quite sure that it stirred his hot anger and resentment. As he lifts this heavy cross, it is not its weight alone that causes his face to burn. It is rather the anger that he feels from the bearing of such a shameful burden. He is indignant at himself. He realizes that his own curiosity is partly to blame for this humiliating experience. "If you had gone about your own business," he mutters to himself, "this would never have happened to you." But his condemnation of himself is mild in comparison with that he feels against these soldiers and against the bullying nation of which they are a part. In his fierce anger he is half minded to throw this cross down and to defy these bloody men, even though it cost him his life. But he is sane enough to realize that such a course would be madness. Therefore, he takes up this burden and stalks forward with a resentment that kindles the very fires of hell within his heart.

Then along with his anger at himself and at Rome, I can well imagine that he has an unreasoning anger against this Prisoner who is unable to bear his own cross. Anger, you know, is seldom reasonable. In our ordinary language we call it getting mad. That is a fitting word. An angry man is in a measure a madman. Therefore Simon looked at Jesus, not with sympathy, but with indignation. Possibly he muttered under his breath, "You can't take it. If you are too weak to bear your own cross, you ought never to have launched upon the kind of life that would bring you to a cross." Thus, full of resentment against Rome, and against this weak Prisoner, he walks toward Calvary about as wretched and bitter a man as there was in that whole city.

But there is good reason to believe that Simon's bitter resentment underwent a change. Something happened that put out the hot fires of his anger. We could hardly have believed that such a change was possible. We would never have dreamed that the bleak winter of his soul could so quickly be transformed into blossoming spring. But so it happened. Instead of being dreadfully ashamed of bearing this cross, I imagine that he came to take an actual pride in the bearing of it. Instead of a burning desire to throw down his burden, I have a fancy that he found his hated task transformed into a privilege.

III

How, I wonder, has this change been wrought?

We may be sure that it was Jesus that made the first move in this direction. No sooner had Simon lifted that cross to his shoulders than Jesus began to speak to him. Whether he spoke to him in words we do not know. If he did so, those words are not recorded. But we may be sure that he spoke in a language more compelling than words. He spoke through his own radiant and winsome personality. Drummond tells us that in the heart of Africa, among the great lakes, he came across black men and women who remembered the only white man they had ever seen before. That man was David Livingstone. He said further that their dark faces would light up as they spoke of the kind Doctor that passed that way years ago. They could not understand a word that he said. But somehow they felt the love that beat in the heart of him.

If Livingstone made this impression, how much greater must have been the impression made by Livingtone's Master!

But though the record does not tell us that Jesus said anything to Simon, I love to imagine that he did. It would have been so like him. Look at the picture: Simon, hot and angry, is shouldering the cross. Jesus looks into the scowling face and says softly, "I am sorry to have to trouble you like this. You know I am not quite up to myself today." Simon, startled by these words, is still more startled as he hears himself saying, "That's all right. I myself am feeling very fit. I can carry it well enough. It is not so heavy for one who has not bled as you have."

So the procession moves on till they come to the foot of the hill called Calvary. Then the Master speaks to Simon again. "It has been very good of you to carry my load for me, but we are almost there. I can manage the rest of the way." But I have an idea that Simon's heart has now begun to burn within him with a glad joy that he has never felt before. He feels that he is really helping this Man. Not only so, but he feels that in helping him he is doing something that is of supreme worth. Somehow it dawns upon him, dimly at first, that in serving this strange Prisoner he is helping the whole world. He therefore resolves to keep on at all cost.

For this reason he refuses to surrender his once unwelcome burden. "The hill is a bit steep," he says;

"I will carry it to the top for you." Having done this, Simon doubtless stands by to the very end. And I should not wonder that Jesus found the cross a bit easier because of the presence of this conscript who has become a friend. When all is over, when he has heard Jesus saying, "Father, into thy hands I commend my spirit," then he goes his way. But that cross that he has once borne in bitterness, he now takes up willingly to bear for the remainder of his days. Thus what had once been his shame has become his supreme boast. In fact, I am sure that he came to say with Paul, "God forbid that I should glory, save in the cross of our Lord Jesus Christ." We are confident that through this experience Simon became a new creation in Christ Jesus.

Not only did this experience set Simon's feet on the road to newness of life, but it made him an unmeasured blessing to others. When he got back home he had a wonderful story to tell. There were two small boys in that home named Rufus and Alexander. When these boys climbed upon their father's knee to ask for a story, he had one to tell that was so fresh and wonderful that their childish eyes sparkled and their hearts grew big with joy. No wonder these two small boys listened to this story with intense interest. No wonder that they had their father tell it again and again. It was then, and still is, the sweetest story ever told. When Simon had finished telling how this Man of the cross had won him and had accepted him as his very own, quite naturally these boys asked, "Will he take little chaps like us too?" And the father answered with tenderness and tears, "Indeed he will. He said, 'Suffer the little children to come unto me.'" Therefore, we are not surprised that when Mark tells the story years later he mentions among the saints these two boys now grown to useful manhood. Thus as Simon co-operated with God, he found life abundant both for himself and for others as well.

VII

THE FALSE FRIEND

"Judas Iscariot, who became a traitor."

LUKE 6:16

❋

OF ALL THE FACES THAT WE SEE ABOUT THE CROSS, there is none other quite so tragic as that of Judas. Not only is his a tragic face, but it is one that is vastly baffling and perplexing. This is evidenced by the fact that those who look into that face do not always come away with the same impression. A few see in Judas a blundering and mistaken hero, but the vast majority see only an inhuman scoundrel. These latter shut their eyes to all the good that was in him. They remember only one single act of his pathetic pilgrimage, his betrayal of his Lord. This, it seems to me, is not quite fair. Therefore, I am going to ask you to look at him again, forgetting for the present, so far as possible, the one black blot upon his life.

I

About this man Judas I think we may safely make three simple assertions.

1. Judas was not a monster, but a man. He was just as human as ourselves. This sounds trite, I know, but such is not in reality the case. We who are decent and respectable are constantly prone to look upon those who go vastly wrong as being entirely different from ourselves. They are made of the slime and ooze of things, while we are made of far finer material. It is hard for us to realize our kinship with one who betrayed his Lord. For instance, G. Campbell Morgan is easily one of the great expository preachers of our day. Many have both heard and read him to their enlightenment and edification. Listen to what he has to say about this false friend of Jesus. "I do not believe that Judas was a man in the ordinary sense of the word. I believe that he was a devil incarnate, created in history for the nefarious work that was hell's work."

There have no doubt been many through the centuries who have felt this way about Judas. But, of course, we cannot agree. Such an explanation raises far more questions than it settles. If Judas were created an incarnate devil, if he were sent into the world to be a traitor to Jesus, then he is not to blame for being what he was, and doing what he did. He is no more to blame than the vessel that has been spoiled by the potter is to blame.

> "They sneer at me for leaning all awry:
> What! did the Hand then of the Potter shake?"

Who under these circumstances is to blame? The only answer is God. But this view we cannot accept. God never created any man either a monster or a devil. Traitors and scoundrels are not born, but made. We must, therefore, believe that Judas was a man.

2. Not only do we assume that Judas was thoroughly human, but we assume further that he was not always a traitor. Luke tells us that he became a traitor. He was certanly not born with the guilt of treachery upon his baby soul. When his mother looked the love light into his eyes in his young and tender years, she saw no treachery there. No more was he a traitor in the early days of his fellowship with Jesus. I know that there are those who say that he was a devil from the beginning. But the Scriptures make no such assertion. In John 6:70 Jesus says, "Have I not chosen you, the Twelve, and one of you is a devil?" The real meaning of this latter clause is: "One of you is devilish." So spoke Jesus of Judas one year before the betrayal. At that time Judas was facing in the wrong direction. But even then Jesus does not mean to say that he is wholly bad. Judas never became wholly bad. The fact that his ghastly deed filled him with such utter

horror shows that there was still much good in him. A man entirely dead to goodness would not have acted as did Judas.

When Jesus therefore said that Judas was devilish he was only saying what we often say about one another. His criticism was certainly no sharper than that he spoke personally to Simon Peter. This disciple had just risen to great heights. He had said to Jesus, "Thou art the Christ, the Son of the living God." The Master had replied with great enthusiasm, "Blessed art thou; for flesh and blood hath not revealed it unto thee, but my Father who is in heaven." But a moment later, when this same disciple was warning his Master against accepting the Cross, when he was saying, "Be it far from me, Lord," Jesus turned upon him and said, "Get thee behind me, Satan." It was a sharp and cutting word. But it did not mean that Simon was wholly bad. No more does the Master's sharp word about Judas mean that he is beyond hope. Judas became a traitor, but he was not so from the beginning.

3. I think we can only assume that Judas was not always a traitor, but that he was at one time a loyal friend. For this view there are certain arguments that are very convincing.

First, there is the fact that Judas was a disciple of Jesus. He began to follow the Master before he was chosen as an apostle. He followed Jesus of his own choice. How these two met we are not told. But one day they stood face to face. One day they looked into each other's eyes. Perhaps Judas had stood on the fringe of a crowd and heard this strange Prophet speak. He had heard him say, "If any man will come after me, let him deny himself." The conditions seemed hard to one like Judas, who was evidently a lover of money. But in spite of that fact, Judas forsook his business to become a disciple. This amazing Man cast a spell over him that he found it impossible to resist.

There are those who suggest that while Judas became a disciple he did so from mixed motives. He was not altogether unselfish. He was not seeing eye to eye with his Lord. Granted. But if we go into the realm of motives, who can stand? Certainly not ourselves, certainly not the fellow-disciples of Judas. James and John came one day, you remember, hiding behind their mother's skirts to ask for positions of particular honor in the Kingdom. Their fellow-disciples were filled with indignation. This was the case, not because they were horrified at their mixed motives, but because, being of mixed motives themselves, they were grasping for the same prize that was being sought by James and John. I believe that Judas was at one time friendly, because of his own choice he became a follower of Jesus.

Second, I believe that Judas was at one time a friend, not only because he chose to follow the Master, but because that Master chose him to be an apostle. Jesus did not have to choose him. There were others, some of them quite worthy, whom he might have selected in the place of this man. Why then did he choose him? I am sure that he did not choose him because he was a rascal. A good man does not choose his closest friends on that basis. No more did he choose him because he saw that he was to be a traitor. He chose him as he chose the other disciples, because he was a man of fine possibilities. He chose him because he had in him the making of a great servant and a great saint.

Finally, I think that we may be sure that Judas was at one time a friend because he was so regarded by his fellow-disciples. They trusted him sufficiently to make him the treasurer of the group. When their Master sent them upon a mission, it is evident that he did his work as well as the rest. If this had not been the case, the Evangelists would doubtless have recorded the fact. They would also, in all probability, have called attention to any indications of treachery if they had known such. But Judas was never suspected. Even at their last meal, when the Master said, "One of you shall betray me," not one looked accusingly at Judas. No one said, "Thou art the man." But with a humility that did not always characterize them, each looked into his own heart and said, "Lord, is it I?" All these reasons tend to prove that Judas was once a loyal friend.

II

How then did Judas become a traitor?

There are those who say that Judas was not in reality a treacherous man at all. They affirm that he was only a mistaken man. They believe that, in spite of his seemingly heartless conduct, he deeply loved Jesus. Not only so, but that he trusted him with a faith more daring than that of any of his fellow-disciples. They declare that he believed in Jesus with such absolute conviction that he was sure that, once it became necessary, the Master would assert his power and set up his Kingdom. In this faith, these affirm, Judas decided to put his Lord on the spot. He determined to create for him a situation where he must exercise his power and assume his role of conqueror.

Naturally, there is not one of us that would not like to believe this. But the trouble is, there is no evidence of its truth. All the evidence points in the opposite direction. The Evangelists never speak of Judas as merely a misguided and mistaken man, but always as a deliberately treacherous man. What is more convincing still, Jesus himself, whose loving eye always saw the best, makes no excuse for Judas. This Man who apologized for the soldiers who murdered him, who threw about them "the sheltering folds of a protecting prayer," "Father, forgive them, for they know not what they do," has no word of excuse for the Traitor. He does not regard him as a man who through misguided zeal did a foolish thing, but as one who through wickedness of heart did a treacherous and devilish thing.

93

How then may we explain Judas? Of course, a full explanation is impossible. We can only guess. Of this we may be sure, there came a day when this follower of Jesus began to face away from him. Judas at some time or another took a false step, and began to travel in the wrong direction. This seemed a small matter at the time, but its end was tragic. I have reminded you before that the direction in which we are traveling is the most important fact about any of us. What we are is of importance, but what we are becoming is of far greater importance. If we are facing in the right direction there is no telling how Christlike we may become, for we have a whole eternity in which to climb. If we are facing in the wrong direction, ever so slightly, there is no telling to what depths we may descend. Judas for some reason took a wrong direction.

As to how he took this false step, we cannot be sure. Judas was the only disciple who was not a Galilean. That, in itself, offered a soil in which the rank weeds of jealousy might grow. Then one day it became clear to Judas that all the apostles did not share equally in the Master's confidence. Jesus was taking certain ones into an inner circle of friendship. This inner circle was composed of blundering Simon and of hot-hearted James and John. Judas, who was perhaps one of the brightest and best trained men of the group, Judas, who thought well of himself, was not included. In all probability this was a keen disappointment to

Judas. Not only so, but it doubtless aroused in him a resentment that grew more bitter with the passing of the days.

This resentment was further increased by the fact that matters were not turning out as Judas had hoped. When he began to follow Jesus, he was sure that the Master was going to establish a temporal and earthly kingdom. That faith he shared along with all the other disciples. Here was a Man who was going to set his people free. He was going to enable his nation to put its foot upon the neck of its foes, to conquer as it had been conquered. But here again he met disappointment. When the Master made his triumphal entry into Jerusalem, when things seemed ripe for a decisive blow, he did nothing more aggressive than weep over the city he should have captured. "Maybe," thought Judas, "he is not to be a conqueror after all."

Thus disappointed in his own personal advancement and in the prospects of a worldly kingdom, Judas had perhaps decided to get out of the mad adventure what little he could. Therefore he began to steal from the common purse. Of course he did not call it stealing. At first he told himself that he would replace the money some day. Then he told himself that what he took was a part payment of his legitimate salary. He was doing most of the work. Besides, the money he took was trifling in proportion to what he could have made had he not given up his business to set out on this wild-goose chase.

While Judas was soothing his conscience by soft lies, while he was deceiving his fellow-disciples, he realized that there was One that he was not deceiving. He felt that Jesus knew him for what he was. He saw disappointment and grief in those kindly eyes that read the very secrets of his soul. Thus he found himself vastly uncomfortable, even wretched in the presence of the Master whose fellowship had once been his comfort and joy. Judas put the blame for this change, not on himself, but on Jesus. Therefore, he came to hate this one-time Friend with a deadly hatred. So intense was his hatred that at last he said to the enemies of Jesus, "What will you give me, and I will deliver him to you?"

What was the price? Thirty pieces of silver. What a trifling sum! It was the price of a slave. No doubt Judas expected far more, but his seducers had him at their mercy. He had betrayed himself into their hands, and there was no going back. Therefore, he took the money because thirty pieces of silver was thirty pieces of silver. But greed was not his primary motive for betraying Jesus. Had such been the case he would not have kissed him. That kiss was more than a finger pointing the Master out to his foes. "He kissed him lavishly," says Mark. There was venom in those kisses. Jealous, disappointed, greedy Judas had come so to hate the man that he once loved, that he could betray him with a kiss.

III

What can we say of the destiny of this pathetic man? On this subject the Bible is tenderly reticent. But there are three words that we may notice briefly.

1. There is the word of Simon Peter. He tells us that Judas went to his own place. That is delicately stated. He does not affirm that this false friend plunged into the eternal night. He only says that he went out to meet the destiny that he had prepared for himself. We enter the door, each of us, for which we are ready. If we prepare ourselves for the companionship of the holiest and best, into that companionship we shall surely go. If we prepare ourselves for the companionship of those who hate the best and love the worst, even into that companionship we shall go also. We go each to his own place. So it was with Judas. Wherever traitors are at home, there we may expect to find this man.

2. Then there is the word of Jesus. What did Jesus think of the destiny of this false friend? Before the betrayal Jesus knew that Judas was not his friend. But he refused to dismiss him. He knew that if love and patience could not save him, ostracism and indifference would surely fail. But Judas made it impossible for the Master to realize his holy purpose for him. Therefore, in his last prayer Jesus says this revealing word: "Those that thou hast given me I have kept, and none of them is lost, but the son of perdition." "The son of perdition"—that is Judas. And Jesus

says with infinite heartache, "I have lost him." There can be no more tragic word than that.

3. Finally, there is the verdict of Judas himself. After this kiss, Judas expected to go his way. But this he cannot do. A fatal fascination draws him to the trial. There he hears the Man that he has betrayed sentenced to death. Then a terrible reaction sets in. It is awful to think of the suffering of this desperate man. The very flames of hell are kindled in his heart. Infinitely the most awful hour of his life is upon him. He has needed help before, but never has his need been so crushing as now.

Where does he turn in his hour of need? That is a searching question. The answer to that will give us a look into the very heart of the man. Where do we go when the skies are black, and when life for us has fallen into ruins? We seek help from varied sources. Some turn to drink. Some turn to God. But Judas in this hour of need turns, not to Jesus, but to the heartless devils that have wrecked him. I can conceive of no more revealing nor tragic fact than that. It shows us the effect of Judas' sin upon himself. It has so blinded him to the mercy and goodness of Jesus that at his blackest hour he sees more hope in the worst of men than in Love Incarnate. There can be no hotter hell than that. And this blindness is a danger that threatens, not Judas alone, but every one of us. We can refuse to see till our eyes go out.

VIII

MISTAKEN TEARS

"Daughters of Jerusalem, weep not for me, but weep for yourselves, and for your children."

LUKE 23:28

I

IF EVER THERE WAS A JUST CAUSE FOR TEARS, IT would seem to be here. Jesus with two robbers is on his way to Calvary. The streets are jammed with curious crowds. These crowds are for the most part hostile, especially to Jesus. They seem to have a resentment for his weakness. They find it easy to ridicule and insult the Man who threatens at any moment to fall under the weight of his too heavy cross. But while these faces are for the most part unfriendly, there are some exceptions. There are a few women who are sorry for this Man who is being led to such a ghastly death. "He is so innocent," they whisper one to the other. "Yes, and so young. Why, he is almost a boy." Therefore they are so sorry for him that they burst into tears.

The reaction of Jesus to those tears is at first a bit surprising. He does not seem to appreciate them. Yet, no other man was ever quite so appreciative as He. No other was ever quite so sensitive to kindness. He declared that even one who gave so much as a cup of cold water in his name would be sure of a reward. Less than a week ago a young woman at a dinner party showed him a kindness. It was a rather silly kindness, in the opinion of Judas, as expensive as it was useless. Yet, Jesus appreciated it, called it beautiful, and declared that her name should be linked with his own to the end of time. "Wheresoever this gospel shall be preached throughout the whole world, this also that she hath done shall be spoken of for a memorial of her." Yet he shows no appreciation of the tears of these wailing women.

Why, I wonder, is this the case? I think it is true for at least two reasons. First, Jesus has a strong man's natural aversion to being pitied. If you enjoy having your fellows pity you, there is very likely something radically wrong with you. But the supreme reason why Jesus does not appreciate these tears is because he sees that these women have missed the real point of the tragedy. He sees that theirs are mistaken tears. There are some folks who have no sense of

humor. They laugh not at all. Or they have a per-
verted sense of humor and laugh at the wrong time
and at the wrong things. Even so, there are those who
do not know when or for what reason they ought to
weep. These women are perfectly right in shedding
tears. But they are weeping for the wrong cause.
They are sobbing over Jesus when they ought to be
sobbing over themselves and their children.

It is in a sense a tribute to our conception of Jesus
that we can today hear such a word without laughing.
We hear it with our ears enlightened by nineteen centuries of history. But how utterly absurd this word
must have sounded to those who first heard it. Look
at that great crowd. Who is the most tragic figure
among them? Of course there are two robbers who
are to die, but they are hard inside and out. They
seem able to take it. There is the thoughtless multitude. They are a bit pathetic, but seemingly not pitiful
enough for tears. Then there is Annas with his crowd.
Surely they are least of all to be pitied. They are winning an easy victory. A few hours from now they will
return to their homes congratulating themselves upon
the fact that they have put this young Carpenter, who
was threatening to become troublesome, out of the
way. It is easy to see who is the most tragic figure in
this crowd. It is surely that lonely young Prophet who
set out a few months ago with such high dreams and
holy purposes, but who is now finding all these blighted
by a grim and horrible cross.

But Jesus had a different reading of things. Even most of us, in spite of our blindness, I think agree with him today. If you had to be some one of the characters about the cross, I think you would certainly choose to be this doomed Prophet. Be that as it may, it is evident that Jesus does not count himself an object of pity. He declares rather that the pitiable ones are the women themselves. They are the people as a whole who have turned against him and are helping to do him to death. They are above all the religious leaders who in their self-chosen blindness are crucifying the Prince of Life. No wonder, therefore, that Jesus cries, "Weep not for me, but weep for yourselves, and for your children. . . . . For a time is coming when they shall say to the mountains, Fall on us; and to the hills, Cover us." The Master is here asserting that the one something of supreme importance is the attitude of men toward himself. He is declaring that a wrong attitude can end for those who take it only in dire tragedy. He is asserting that, in crucifying him, these and all others, are in consequence crucifying both themselves and their children.

These are startling words. They are so startling that they sound like a strange tongue to our ears. Multitudes today believe that while a man's attitude toward Jesus may be of some importance, it is not necessarily of supreme importance. The idea that God might punish a man for his rejection of His Son is foreign to our thinking. Hell, about which our fathers spoke with such passionate vehemence, has so cooled that it would now be a fairly good summer resort. God our Father is good. In fact, he is so good that he threatens to become goody-goody. "Do you think," one asks indignantly, "that a loving God would send any man, even the worst, to hell?" "No," I answer; "I do not think so, yet I am sure that there are a good many that are living in a hell of their own making." I might ask a question that is equally reasonable: "Do you think that God will punish a man for a false belief?" "Certainly not," you reply. Yet I knew a man recently who became convinced that he could live without eating and drinking. To all appearances he was absolutely sincere. He bet his life on his false faith. But in spite of the goodness of God and the sincerity of his faith, he became first a walking skeleton, then he fainted and went into a coma. All that saved him from death was forced feeding.

It is written into the constitution of things that the man who refuses to obey the laws of physical health must suffer. It is no less written into the constitution of things that the man who refuses to obey the laws of spiritual health must suffer also. If when we neglect to take bread we die, even so we die spiritually when we fail to avail ourselves of the Bread of Life. And there is no forced feeding here. We must take this Bread of our own choice. This is not mere theory; this is plain everyday fact. It is true for the individual. It is true for the group. It is true for the world. Men judge themselves in the presence of Jesus. He is the way, the truth, and the life. To miss him is to miss the way. To miss the way is to arrive at a wrong goal. To miss the truth is to believe a lie. "If a lie is built into a rock wall," says Carlyle, "that wall will fall down." So also will the individual, society, the world. He is the life. To have him is to have life. To miss him is to grip the frozen hand of death.

If you do not believe this, look at the individual. Look perchance into your own heart. Just in proportion that you have missed him, you have missed life. Look abroad at our world. We are living in one of the most tragic eras in all history. Our whole world is sick. What is the matter? The symptoms are endless. But there is only one disease. We have rejected God. We have crucified our Lord. By so doing we are crucifying ourselves and our world. There is not a single evil that vexes society today that could not be cured, given sufficient loyalty to Christ. That is the conviction not simply of the saints. Even Bernard Shaw, an unbeliever, declares as much. Thus we see that the supreme tragedy, the one matter for tears, is rejection of Jesus Christ. This is true regardless of the method of our rejection. Some reject him aggressively and cruelly, as did these Jews of the long ago. Some reject him passively, decently, with very courteous respect. But the method does not signify. The fact alone is what matters. "How shall we escape if we neglect . . . ." There is no escape.

"When Jesus came to Golgotha they hanged him on a
    tree,
  They drave great nails through hands and feet, and
    made a Calvary;
  They crowned him with a crown of thorns; red were
    his wounds and deep,
  For those were crude and cruel days, and human flesh
    was cheap.

"When Jesus came to our town, they simply passed
    him by;
  They never hurt a hair of him, they only let him die;
  For men had grown more tender, and they would not
    give him pain;
  They only just passed down the street, and left him
    in the rain." [1]

II

But, facing his own seemingly tragic situation, Jesus says, "Weep not for me." What he is saying is this: "I am not to be pitied. I am rather to be congratulated." Why is this the case?

1. He is to be congratulated because he is within the will of God. He has asked above all else that He might be privileged to do God's will. This is the answer to that prayer. Therefore as he goes his lonely way he is conscious of the fact that he is right with God and right with himself. Obeying God, he is enjoying the fellowship of God. "He that hath sent me is with me. The Father hath not left me alone, because I

---

[1] From "Indifference," by G. A. Studdert-Kennedy, in *The Sorrows of God*. Used by permission of Harper & Brothers.

do always the things that please him." Living within the will of God, and possessing God, he possesses all things. He has even now a place that passeth all understanding. No man can ever be pitiable who is thus conscious of the fact that he is right.

But you say it is costing him everything. It is costing him poverty, even death. So it is. But in spite of that he is to be congratulated. I know some find it hard to believe this. One of the sins of our age is softness. Too many of us are convinced that the worst that can befall anyone is for that one to have a hard time. Here, for instance, are two business men. All of us have known them both. They meet financial disaster. Both lose all that they possess and more. But they do not face the calamity in the same fashion. One of them dreads poverty more than he dreads dishonesty. Therefore, he becomes a creature of shifts and devices. He manages to go bankrupt and yet leave himself a comfortable fortune. He continues to live as he did when he was prosperous. He lives in the same house, drives the same lovely cars. Quite a keen chap, some fancy, even if he is carrying on at the expense of his creditors. But the other man is rather dull. In fact, he is so stupid that he turns over every dollar he has to his creditors. "I am sorry I cannot pay you one hundred cents on the dollar," he apologizes. "But if God spares me, some day I will." Poor fellow! He has no better sense than to do what is right.

Yet, Jesus would not pity this man. He would congratulate him.

2. Then Jesus thought himself worthy of congratulation because he is doing the thing that he most longs to do. Those wailing women think the cross is being forced upon his weak shoulders. They think that his rich life is being wrenched out of his hands. Jesus knows they are wrong. "I do not have to bear the cross," he says. "I am bearing it of my own choice. I am not losing my life, I am giving it. 'No man taketh it from me, but I lay it down of myself.' I have found something big enough to live for, and big enough to die for. For the joy that is set before me I am enduring the cross and despising the shame. Therefore congratulate me." Is not this a very sane word, however it may contradict our popular belief and our selfish inclinations? Is it not true that all the really joyous folks are those that of their own choice are taking upon themselves the burdens that nobody has a right to ask them to carry? Therefore, to weep over such is to shed stupid and mistaken tears.

3. Finally, Jesus forbids their tears because he is living victoriously. I am aware of the fact that if ever a man seemed defeated it is Jesus. He had set out for no lesser purpose than the redemption of the world. At first he was popular. Great multitudes thronged his steps. But now his popularity has changed into hot hate and bitter antagonism. What a pathetic failure! Yet, only a few hours ago Jesus said, "Be of good

cheer; I have overcome the world." Even now, he is
a conqueror. Not only so, but he is going on conquer-
ing through the endless ages. Soon His enemies will
lift him upon a cross. But that will not be the end.
Lifted up from the earth, he will still draw all men
unto himself. He is possessed of a quality of life that
nothing can destroy; neither evil men, nor death itself.
Since Jesus therefore is within the will of God, since
he is doing the task that he supremely loves, since he
is winning and knows that he will go on winning forever—surely that is not a matter for tears, but for
song and congratulation.

III

"Weep not for me, but weep for yourselves, and for
your children." This is a word that many of us need
today quite as much as those wailing women of long
ago. Our tears are often as mistaken as theirs. We
need to discover our Lord's sense of values that we
may know when to laugh and when to weep. It is
significant that Jesus, when he wept over his fellows
because of the horrible tragedy that he saw was ahead
of them, wept over his enemies, never over his friends.
"And when he was come near, he beheld the city, and
wept over it, saying, If thou hadst known, even thou, at
least in this thy day, the things which belong unto thy
peace! but now they are hid from thine eyes. For the
days shall come upon thee, that thine enemies shall cast a
trench about thee, and compass thee round, and keep

thee in on every side." Who are these that wrung from Jesus this gush of bitter tears? They were those who were rejecting him. They were not his friends, they were his enemies.

But while Jesus wept over his enemies, he never wept in such fashion over his friends. This is true in spite of the fact that he saw for them physical suffering as real as that which he saw for his enemies. There was a tragedy, therefore, ahead for these enemies that was far deeper than that of physical death. We can be sure of this because when Jesus foretold the persecution of his friends he did not weep. He did not show the slightest emotion when he told one of his dearest disciples by what death he should glorify God. In fact, he seemed to feel that such tragedy was almost nothing at all. He never once prayed for exemption for his friends any more than he did for himself. "I pray not that thou shouldest take them out of the world, but that thou shouldest keep them from the evil." His one prayer for them as for himself was this: "Thy will be done." He knew that everything works for good to the man that is within the will of God.

In the first century two young men heard the appeal of Jesus. These had much in common. They were both choice and gifted. One of them, Stephen by name, was so taken captive by Jesus that he threw himself into his service with passionate devotion. He stirred up such hot antagonism that he was publicly mobbed, and his battered young body was laid in an untimely grave.

The other man was one that we call the Rich Young Ruler. Jesus cast such a spell over him that one day he left his palace to run down the road and kneel in his presence. When Jesus saw how fine and clean he was, it is said that he loved him. In his eagerness to give him the best, he said, "Go thy way, sell whatsoever thou hast, and give to the poor, and thou shalt have treasure in heaven: and come, follow me." But the price was higher than the young man was willing to pay. Therefore, we read of him this sentence: "He went away." Thus he refused to squander his life as did Stephen. He was wise enough to keep his head and not to let his emotions get the better of him.

Now I am going to imagine that these two, Stephen and the Young Ruler, were friends. I am going to imagine further that they had a mutual friend who loved them both. Forty years have gone by, let us say, since Stephen was martyred. Today this mutual friend is visiting the Rich Ruler, who is no longer young, but is now a rich and gracious old man. "While in Jerusalem the other day," says this friend, "I decided to visit the grave of Stephen. You know I expected to have a hard time finding it, but it was no trouble at all. There was a well-worn path leading to it. Besides, there were upon it some flowers that were fresh as the morning. But as I stood there I could hardly keep back the tears as I thought of how much Stephen missed. He has been dead now for forty years. He threw his life away, it seems to me, for just nothing at all. But as I grieved over him, I rejoiced over you. For I thought how near that same fanatical Carpenter came to getting you. I would not have given much for your chance that day you ran down and kneeled at his feet. But when he asked you to give away your money you saw through him. You always had a pretty good eye for money. I bet you have congratulated yourself on your escape a thousand times."

But the Rich Old Ruler shakes his head slowly and looks at his visitor through tired eyes. "No," he said, "you are mistaken. I have not congratulated myself, not once. I was disappointed the day I turned my back on Jesus. I have been disappointed ever since. I have never been able to get away from a feeling that in so doing I missed the best. I am sure that Stephen used his life better than I have used mine. You and I were by, you remember, when Stephen died. He had a light in his face, even in death, that I have never been able to forget. Somehow I have a conviction that one moment of light like that would be worth a whole life lived in the twilight as I have lived mine. No, don't congratulate me, congratulate Stephen." The Ruler was right. There is but one superlative tragedy; that is to miss knowing God through Christ. There is but one matter for highest congratulation; that is to know Him whom to know aright is life eternal. He is our only hope for the life that now is as well as for that which is to come. May God help us to believe it.

IX

PILATE THE COWARD

"When Pilate heard that saying, he was more afraid."

JOHN 19:8

❋

HE WAS THE MORE AFRAID." THEN THIS WAS NOT the first time that the weakening fingers of fear had clutched at Pilate's heart. From the beginning of this unwelcome trial Pilate had been afraid. This, I dare say, he would never have confessed even to himself. He was a Roman official with a huge contempt for the people that he had been sent to govern. Had anyone accused him of cowardice he would have gnashed his teeth with shame and rage. Had anyone convinced him that his one claim to immortality would be for an act of cowardice, he would have been amazed beyond all words. Yet, such is the case. From generation to generation we remind ourselves of his coward's deed when we say, "He suffered under Pontius Pilate."

Because Pilate was more weak than wicked we find it impossible to think of him as we do some of those who shared with him in this memorable crime. We cannot think of him, for instance, as we do of Annas, that cunning spider, who had grown old in trickery and cruelty. He spun his web without the slightest regard for right and wrong. We cannot think of him as we think of Caiaphas, the High Priest. Pilate had a conscience. He had a sense of justice. He was eager to do the right thing by his Prisoner. He would have done the right thing under circumstances less compelling. There is no doubt that the face of this haughty Roman Governor was the friendliest into which Jesus looked at this trial. But Pilate lacked the courage of his convictions. He was a bit of a weakling. Therefore, we feel sorry for him. We find ourselves wishing that we could help him. We could even weep over him if we could find any tears bitter enough.

To be convinced that Pilate's failure was born of weakness and cowardice it is only necessary to examine the facts.

I

The first scene of this tragedy gives us hope. The time is early Friday morning, the place is a space called the Pavement, between the wings of the palace.

From the beginning of this trial, which was destined to be the most memorable in all history, Pilate seemed to be in a bad mood. There were varied circumstances connected with the case that tended to irritate him. In the first place, he was perhaps routed out of bed earlier in the morning than was his custom. Then he was doubtless somewhat familiar with the history of the Prisoner that he was called to examine. What he had heard made him unwilling to judge the case. More irritating still was the fact that these contemptible Jews would not enter his palace lest they should be defiled. They, the conquered subjects that he had been sent to rule, felt themselves better than himself, a Roman Governor. It is not surprising, therefore, that there was a heavy scowl on his face when he had to go outside to them instead of their coming to him.

Then Pilate was further irritated by incidents connected with the trial. When he opened the proceedings with the routine question, "What charges bring you against this man?" they refused to name the crime with which he was charged. Instead they answered, "If he were not a criminal, we would not have brought him to you." That was no way to answer a Roman Governor. But they were telling Pilate without mincing words that they themselves had examined the Prisoner and had found him guilty. Pilate then, thinking the charge was the infringement of some bit of their nonsensical ritual, said, "Take him and judge him according to your law." Here Pilate tried to stifle a yawn and get the troublesome matter off his hands. But the answer of these Jewish leaders continued to be thoroughly irritating. "We are not allowed to put a man to death," they reply. By this they are daring to tell Pilate that they have not only found the Prisoner guilty, but that they have sentenced him to death. He is to die on the cross. "You must crucify him," they imply, "whether you think him guilty or innocent, whether you think the sentence just or unjust."

When Pilate heard that they had sentenced Jesus to death, he realized the nature of the accusation that they were bringing against him. They were accusing him of treason. They were claiming that he was setting himself up as a rival to Caesar. Pilate did not believe this. But he dared not refuse an investigation. He was none too well established in the good graces of Tiberius already. Therefore, he had Jesus brought into the palace. He was too wise to undertake the examination in the presence of the mob. It was in this room in the palace that Pilate doubtless came face to face with his Prisoner for the first time. That the Governor did not find Jesus the kind of man he expected is clearly evident. We can read his vast amazement between the lines. "Thou," he said in awed wonder, "art thou a King?" Pilate had never seen a pretender that looked like this Man. He felt at once that he was no rival of Caesar. Yet, in his presence he was strangely afraid.

Listen to the answer that Jesus made to the Governor's question as to his being a King: "Sayest thou this thing of thyself, or did others tell it thee of me?" Pilate, are you speaking out of your own experience, or from hearsay? Jesus has forgotten Pilate, the Governor. He is thinking only of Pilate, the man. The Good Shepherd is out in quest of this sheep that is lost. He is trying to save this man, in whom there was so much good, from the terrible tragedy that he sees ahead of him."

Pilate is astonished at Jesus' answer. "Am I a Jew?" he replies. "Your own nation has condemned you; what have you done?" Then the Master makes another effort to help Pilate. "I am a king," he declares. "But my kingdom is not of this world. It is not founded on force like that of Caesar. If such were the case, my servants would have fought. But I am a king in the realm of the Truth. To this end was I born, and for this cause came I into the world, that I might bear witness to the Truth." And here Jesus held open the door into his kingdom for bewildered Pilate. But though the Governor has not the courage to enter, he is greatly impressed. "What is truth?" he answers. Pilate was not jesting here as Bacon suggests. He was never more serious in his life. Having in desperaton asked this question, he waited not for an answer, but went out to render his verdict.

What had Pilate to say as to the guilt or innocence of the Prisoner? He has not been sufficiently convinced of Jesus' kingship in the realm of Truth to enter that kingdom. But he has reached a verdict as to his guilt or innocence of the charge of treason. It was a verdict in which he was perfectly honest and sincere. Had Pilate been so minded he could have declared Jesus guilty and been strictly true to the letter of the law. Jesus himself had declared that he was a king. But Pilate was too honest to see in this man a rival of Caesar. Therefore, when he took his seat in the place of judgment, he declared, "We find the defendant not guilty!"

II

So far we must agree that Pilate has conducted himself as becomes a Roman Governor. But from here on he begins to fail. From here on he allows his weakness to issue more and more into wickedness. When he announces his verdict it is not met by applause. It is met by howls. Pilate sees at once that if he stands by his verdict, he will make strong and unscrupulous enemies. This he is unwilling to do. Therefore, he permits himself to be driven back step by step, not by his convictions, but by numbers and noise.

As the Governor listens to the howls of rage, one voice rings out above all others: "He has stirred up the people all the way from Galilee." Ah, here is a word that sounds like a bit of music in the midst of harsh discord. That is the word Galilee. If the Prisoner is a Galilean, then he belongs to Herod's jurisdiction. Pilate sees in this fact a door through which he may be able to escape. He will send his prisoner to Herod. He will let Herod pass sentence. Thus he will shift his unwelcome responsibility to other shoulders. Thus he will relieve himself of the danger of standing by his honest convictions.

The plan is no sooner thought of than it is put into execution. Jesus is sent to Herod. As he passes from view, Pilate probably dusts off his hands and tells himself that he has got well out of an embarrassing situation. Or he may have been a little more honest than this. He may have sighed a bit wistfully and said, "The Prisoner certainly is innocent. I ought to have set him free, whether these troublesome Jews liked it or not. It is a judge's business to mete out justice whether men throw mud at him or throw bouquets at him." But whether Pilate congratulates or rebukes himself for his conduct, he soon learns that the case is not closed. Herod is interested in Jesus only as a sleight-of-hand performer. When he finds that the Prisoner will not amuse him in this fashion, he sends him back to Pilate. And the Roman Governor still has his chance to be just. He still has an opportunity to stand by his honest convictions. Though, through his weakness, he has lost some ground, he may yet, if he will, save himself from an immortality of shame.

But Pilate still clings to the hope of remaining neutral. He still tries to shift his responsibility to the shoulders of others. He becomes therefore a creature

of schemes and devices. He decides that he will let
the mob decide the question. With this in view, he
reminds the Jews of the fact that they have the privilege
of asking for the release of any prisoner they choose.
But now he does not offer them an unlimited choice.
They must choose between the two. To make sure
that they will ask for the Prisoner that he desires to
release, he selects as an alternative choice the worst prisoner that he knows. He is a revolutionist and a murderer. His name also is Jesus. "Which will you
choose?" he questions hopefully, "Jesus Barabbas or
Jesus the Christ?"

Here it is thought there was an interruption. A
slave hurries through the crowd, kneels at the feet of
Pilate, and offers him a tablet. It is a letter from his
wife, Claudia. Pilate reads the letter with puckered
brows. "Have nothing to do with this just man," it
warns, "for I have suffered many things this day in
a dream because of him." Dreams meant much to the
Romans. Pilate finds the letter disturbing. Meanwhile, the High Priests and their party pass the word
to the mob that they are to ask for the release of Jesus
Barabbas. "Which will you have," questions Pilate
when he has finished the letter, "Jesus the Christ or
Jesus Barabbas?" The answer is thunderous in its
volume, "Jesus Barabbas!"

Pilate is now angry and threadbare in patience. He
would like to act with decision, but does not dare. He
is becoming more and more unmanned. "What shall

I do then with Jesus who is called Christ?" he asks desperately. Into what a tragic position he has allowed them to put him! He has to ask the mob for permission to do an act of justice. He has to ask others what answer he is to give to that question that is so important, and so peculiarly personal. For, in spite of Herod, in spite of the mob, Jesus is on Pilate's hands. Pilate must, therefore, answer this question for himself. He cannot possibly put the responsibility on the shoulders of the crowd.

"What shall I do then with Jesus who is called Christ?" That is your question and mine, as well as that of Pilate. It is intensely personal for us. We cannot shirk it. We cannot remain neutral. We can no more remain neutral toward Christ than we can remain neutral toward the multiplication table. We can no more remain neutral toward him than we can remain neutral to the law of gravitation or to the law of sowing and reaping. Every man of us has Christ on his hands. We must decide for him or we must decide against him. God pity us when we try to pass that responsibility to anyone else. God pity us especially when, as Pilate, we try to leave the answer to the mob. If this question is to be decided aright, we alone can give that decision. Pilate, by trying to shift his responsibility, takes his first downward step.

III

Then Pilate takes a second cowardly step. He decides upon a middle course. He will offer a compromise measure. "I will not be out and out for this Prisoner," he seems to say. "No more will I be out and out against him. Since I have pronounced him not guilty, it is, of course, my duty to release him. But since you Jews are so opposed to this, I am not going to insist on doing what I ought to do. But the fact that I am not going to set him free does not mean that I am consenting to the despicable deed that you desire at my hands. I may not be entirely just, but I certainly am no murderer. Therefore I am not going to kill him. I am going to take a middle course. I am going to half kill him. I will scourge him and let him go."

Now scourging was a terrible torture. Not a few died under the lash. It might be the case with Jesus. But in spite of this Pilate turns him over to the soldiers to be scourged. What strange justice for one whom the Governor has again and again pronounced innocent. The soldiers do their work well. Not only so, but they exceed their orders by putting on the brow of the Prisoner a crown of thorns. It was all so unjust, cruel, and horrible that Pilate hopes that the sight of this tortured Prisoner may satisfy the blood-lust even of this mad mob. Therefore he leads Jesus before them again, saying, "Behold the man." "You have desired to see this Man suffer," he seems to say. "Is not this suffering enough?" But they are not satisfied. Instead, they shrieked only the louder, "Crucify him."

Then they give an added reason for the death sentence:
"He ought to die because he has made himself the Son
of God."

IV

"When Pilate heard that, he was the more afraid."
Pilate is a skeptic. He has broken with the religion
of his own people. He has found no other religion
to take its place. But this amazing Prisoner has impressed him strangely. What if the charge is true?
What if he is the Son of God? He must be sure.
Thus urged on by increasing terror, he goes for a final
interview with Jesus. "Art thou the son of God?" he
asks desperately. But Jesus gives him no answer.
How strange! Pilate is at once amazed and terrified.
Frantically he reminds the Prisoner that he has power
to crucify him and power to let him go. But in spite
of this, the Prisoner answers him never a word. Why
so? Has Jesus grown impatient and angry with this
time-serving governor? No, he simply knows that to
answer Pilate will do no good. When our only response to Truth is a scourge, then the Truth grows
silent to us. If our only response to the Light is to
shut our eyes, then for us the Light refuses to shine.

But in spite of the fact that Jesus has refused to
answer Pilate, the Governor makes one more effort to
save him. He still pronounces his first verdict, "Not
guilty." He is not yet entirely lost. There is still a
slight hope. Then somebody fires the final shot. Then

somebody strikes the fatal blow. I do not know who that somebody else was. I can imagine that it was crafty old Annas. Seeing that the Governor is still fighting, he shouts this deadly word, "If thou let this man go, thou art not Caesar's friend." At that Pilate goes hot and cold. At that his knees become weak. At that his cowardice gains complete mastery. In abject surrender he tosses an innocent man to ghastly death. Thus this haughty Roman Governor earns for himself the ignominious name of Pilate, the Coward.

No wonder the story of Pilate moves us to pity. We cannot but think how differently the story might have ended. For the voice of Annas was not the only voice that was speaking to Pilate at this time. Conscience was speaking to him. A sense of justice and of fair play was speaking to him. They were saying, "If thou let this man go, thou wilt be doing a right deed, a courageous deed." They were saying, "Pilate, you do not have to have the friendship of Caesar. You do not have to keep the position that you now have. But you do have to have the friendship of yourself. You have to live with yourself, and so you ought to be fit for yourself to know." But Pilate makes the blunder of thinking that the friendship of Caesar is more important even than the friendship of right, yes, even than the friendship of God. And let him that is without that same sin cast the first stone at this faltering governor.

And now the deed is done and Jesus is being led away

to his crucifixion. What of Pilate? Does he wring his hands in terror, saying, "Out, out, damned spot"? By no means. There would have been some hope for him if such had been the case. He does indeed wash his hands, but not from any sense of guilt. He rather does so with quiet complacency, saying, "I am innocent of the blood of this just person: see ye to it." He does not even have the courage to face his own guilt. The very light within him has turned to darkness. Had Pilate's crime caused him vast suffering we could have hoped for him. Such suffering would have been a mark of life. But the fact that this deed left him with a quiet conscience is a mark of death. This lack of pain is worse than any anguish, however great. It indicates that Pilate is beyond hope.

X

PILATE THE STUBBORN

"What I have written I have written."

JOHN 19:22

THESE WORDS HAVE AN INTERESTING BACKGROUND. Early Friday morning certain Jewish fanatics routed Pilate out of bed to sit in judgment on a Prisoner. Pilate was unwilling to judge the case, but when he found that the Prisoner was accused of being a pretender he dared not refuse. So he had Jesus brought into the palace where he questioned him personally. From the first he was convinced that here was no rival to Caesar. While the Prisoner declared himself to be a king, he made it clear that he was not a king after the order of the Emperor of Rome. "My kingdom," he declared frankly, "is not of this world: if my kingdom were of this world, then would my servants fight that I should not be delivered to the Jews: but now is my kingdom not from hence."

Pilate was fully convinced of the truthfulness of this declaration. Therefore, he went before the accusers of Jesus with the verdict, "Not guilty." But the Jewish authorities would have none of it. They insisted that the sentence of death be passed. This outraged Pilate's sense of justice. He fought for his own convictions and for the life of his Prisoner. But being more politician than man, he became a creature of shifts and devices. At last he made an abject and unconditional surrender with these words: "Take him, and crucify him: for I find no fault in him."

At this Jesus was turned over to the soldiers. These scourged him, then marched him out to Calvary and nailed him to a cross. According to Roman law, when a man was crucified the crime for which he died must be posted above his head. Pilate therefore did this in the case of Jesus. In Hebrew, Greek, and Latin he wrote the accusation so that all might read. It ran as follows: "Jesus, the King of the Jews."

When the Jewish authorities read this it filled them with rage. They had had Jesus sentenced, not on the grounds that he was in reality a king, but on the grounds that he was a pretender. In pronouncing death sentence Pilate had by that very act declared himself in agreement with the Jews. Therefore, he was not stating the facts as either he himself or the Jews saw them when he wrote, "Jesus, the King of the Jews." For this reason these fanatics were altogether reasonable and within their rights when they came with the modest request that Pilate make the sentence read, not, "Jesus, the King of the Jews," but, "He claimed to be the King of the Jews."

What response did Pilate make to this sane request? Had he been entirely honest he would have said, "You are right, gentlemen. We all agree that Jesus is not in reality a king; he is only a pretender. I will, therefore, have the suggested change made. I do this all the more readily because what is written above the head of a prisoner is of no great importance anyway. The crucified will die just the same whether what I have written is true or false." But, instead of taking this sane position, he became very hot and indignant. He glared at the petitioners angrily. Then he perhaps pounded his fist in his hand and shouted, "I am the Governor, not you. Since I am in authority here, I am not to be pushed about by my own subjects. I have convictions. When I take a position I hold that position at all cost. What I have written I have written."

I

All this sounds very courageous, but what are the facts in the case? Pilate is giving utterance at once to a solemn truth and to a soothing lie. Of the truth he is blissfully unconscious. To the lie he deliberately shuts his eyes.

1. Look, first, at the stern and solemn truth of which he is unconscious. "What I have written I have written," he declares indignantly. How true, Governor, and how terrible! You have done something that you can never undo. You have written a bloody chapter that will be read through the ages, and that neither you nor any other can ever erase. You have given way to compromise. You have done a cowardly and unjust deed. You have crimsoned your hands with the blood of an innocent Man. Face to face with an opportunity to do the big and brave thing, you have done the mean and cowardly thing. Therefore, there is an awful and arresting truth in your declaration, "What I have written I have written."

What Pilate said is a startling word for all of us. "What I have written I have written," is a sentence that befits your lips and mine. Each day brings to us its opportunities, its unsoiled pages. We write our deeds, good and bad, upon these pages. Then the passing day gathers them up and slips through the doorway of the past carrying them forever beyond the reach of our hands. Though we may hammer at that door with bruised fists, though we may tamper at its lock with fingers ever so cunning, we cannot get through the door to make a single change. We face, every one of us, day by day, an unchangeable, irrevocable past.

Just as Pilate we, too, can say, "What I have written I have written."

"The Moving Finger writes; and having writ,
  Moves on; nor all your Piety nor Wit
    Can lure it back to cancel half a line,
  Nor all your Tears wash out a Word of it."

When Pilate, therefore, said this word, he was uttering an awful truth. But it was one of which he was not conscious and about which he was not concerned.

2. But if Pilate was blind to the truth he was uttering, he was little less blind to the lie with which he was trying to soothe his soul. Here is what he is telling himself and his fellows: "I am a brave man. I cannot be pushed about. I cannot be swerved from my determined course. Others may compromise, others may become frightened, others may be browbeaten, but I, the Roman Governor, am not of that type. I am no weakling. I am strong, steadfast, immovable. You can no more brush me from my course than you can brush away the hills that stand about Jerusalem. Therefore, do not try to sway me. What I have written I have written." Having said this, Pilate sends the petitioners away, feeling himself quite sturdy and heroic. But in reality Pilate is not firm and courageous at all. He is merely stubborn.

II

By what right do we say this?

I think we have a right to say it because we can only call that man firm and heroic who stands by his honest convictions. This, Pilate is not doing. The truth is that he has so shut his eyes to the truth that he no longer has convictions. "Pilate, why do you not change the superscription to fit the facts in the case?" And Pilate cannot answer, "I do not change it because I know that I am right. I do not change it because I know that Jesus is really the King of the Jews." Instead, had he dared to tell the truth, he would have said, "What I have written may be false. In fact, I am quite sure that it is false. But that does not matter. I am going to stand by it and brazen it out, not because it is true, but because it is my sentence." It was therefore not heroism, but obstinacy, that caused him to say, "What I have written I have written."

He had, I think, at least two reasons for his stubbornness.

First, he stood by his wrong position because of his eager desire to vex the Jews. These priests with their followers had been to him a constant source of trouble. Pilate had despised them from the beginning. Now he has come to detest them. The hot resentment of other days has been fanned into a flame by the happenings of today. Pilate knows that at this trial he has made a sorry figure. He knows that he has outraged the law that it was his duty to enforce. He blames his collapse on these Jews. This has aroused his keen resentment. Therefore, he writes this sentence and stands by it out of sheer spite. It is his way of getting even with his enemies. Did you ever claim to be firm when in reality you were merely being stubborn out of spite? Few of us, I fear, have been altogether blameless.

Then Pilate was stubborn because he was trying to recover his own self-respect. This Governor had a sense of justice. He represented a strong and sturdy race. But he had struck his flag to the god of noise. He had allowed himself to be driven into doing a mean and dishonorable deed by the howls of the crowd. Shut his eyes how he may, he cannot altogether blind himself to the sorry mess he has made. In order to live with himself in comfort, he feels that he must atone for this in some fashion. But instead of taking the heroic way of confession, he takes the cowardly way of stubbornness. Therefore, when asked to change what he thinks an untrue sentence, he rises in wrath and declares: "I will do nothing of the kind. I am the bravest of the brave. What I have written I have written." Poor, defeated Pilate! In trying to get back some measure of self-respect he seeks to persuade himself that he is firm, when he is only stubborn.

III

Now stubbornness is a common vice. It is as common as it is dangerous. It helped Pilate to his ruin. It may do the same for you and me.

1. This is the case, in the first place, because it is so

easy to mistake stubbornness for a virtue. It is impossible for the average individual to tell the difference between an imitation diamond and the real thing. It is easy for most of us to mistake a string of paste for a string of pearls. In like manner we often get our moral values confused. We sometimes mistake vices for virtues. It is all the easier for us to do this because so many vices are just virtues gone wrong. The partition that divides a virtue from a vice, therefore, is often very thin.

Take the virtue of economy, for instance. Every sane man, I think, realizes the ugliness of wastefulness. To waste is not only bad economy, it is positive sin. One of the darkest blots upon the character of the Prodigal is that he wasted his substance with riotous living. He spent the best for the worst, or for the second best. Neither God nor man has anything to waste. For me to waste money that I have earned is in a most profound sense to waste myself. Money, therefore, is never to be handled carelessly. But, sometimes in our reaction against wastefulness, we react too far. From being merely economical we become downright stingy, even miserly. We become mere getters, seeking to receive all while we give nothing. Such stinginess is a deadly vice. It is all the more dangerous because it is sometimes mistaken for a virtue.

Then there is that beautiful something we call tact. This is a lovely virtue that helps to keep sweet our human relationships. How often I have wished that

I were more tactful. The older I grow the more I
hate to hurt folks. Yet, I realize that often I cause
needless pain, not out of malice, but for the lack of
tact. Yet, as fine as it is to be tactful, I cannot but
realize that this lovely virtue often degenerates into
insincerity and deceit. As much as we enjoy the approval of our fellows, as much as we thrill at being
complimented, there are those whose compliments do
not thrill in the least. What they say may be as sweet
as bonbons dipped in honey, yet they leave us unmoved
because we do not believe they are sincere. In an
effort to be extremely tactful they have become positively deceitful.

Only once, so far as I remember, did I think of the
tactful thing to say before it was too late. At the
close of a service sometime ago, a minister came forward leading two ladies with him. One of these
looked about old enough for his wife, while the other
easily looked old enough to be his mother. "Doctor,"
he said, "I want you to meet my wife." To my surprise the older woman held out her hand. I was sure
that a mistake was being made. Therefore, desiring
to show myself a man of some discernment, I said,
"This is not your wife?" At once I read in the faces
of both indications of an approaching storm. "Yes,
she is my wife too," he answered sternly. "How in
the world," I replied, "did I get it into my head that
you were an old bachelor?" By this answer I saved
their feelings without positive lying. Yet, I am not

sure that I did not color the truth so highly that it amounted to a lie. Thus does the virtue of tact often tend to become the vice of deceit.

Humility is a prize to be coveted. It was one of the fine virtues in himself to which Jesus calls our attention. But what passes for humility may be only a ghastly pretense. Such was the humility of Uriah Heep. Or it may become only an ugly sense of inferiority that burdens its possessor with the curse of self-contempt. Some people are so humble that they refuse all responsibility. There is no load that they can carry, no work that they can do. But, of course, such an attitude is not really humility at all. It is only a sickening caricature of humility. It is the mistaking of an ugly vice for a Christlike virtue. Jesus pronounced a blessing on the poor in spirit, but he had no word of praise for the poor-spirited.

It is even so with stubbornness. It is so easy for us to confuse this ugly vice with the fine virtue of firmness. Firmness is a sound and solid virtue that we cannot but admire. We thrill at the firmness of Daniel as he purposes in his heart that he will not defile himself. We cannot withhold our admiration from Paul as, confronting heavy dangers, he declares, "None of these things move me." We take off our hats to Martin Luther as he faces the perils of his day with the declaration, "Here I stand; I can do no otherwise— God help me." But that which makes the conduct of these men admirable is that they are standing by their reasoned convictions. It is a vastly different matter when we stand with equal steadiness, but have no higher reason than that that actuated Pilate, sheer stubbornness. We need only to look at our own conduct to realize how easy it is for us to flatter ourselves that we are being firm when we are merely being stubborn.

2. Stubbornness is not only dangerous because it often gets itself mistaken for a virtue, but because it tends to close the door of the mind. "Pilate," said these Jews, "what you have written above the cross of Jesus is wrong. You ought to change it." But Pilate refuses to investigate. He refuses to ask whether these Jews are telling the truth or not. The fact is that he is not interested in knowing the truth. He is simply interested in maintaining his position. The stubborn man refuses to face the facts. He does not seek to know the truth. What he has written is right simply because he has written it. He stands by his guns simply because they are his own. He is determined to be consistent even if he is consistently wrong.

3. Stubbornness is dangerous because the stubborn man is always right. Of all the hard folks to live with, none is harder than the one who is never wrong. What havoc such an attitude works in our ordinary relationships. Take the domestic circle, for instance. There is no measuring the harm done by that member of the family that never has to apologize because he is always right. I have in mind a certain father who, years ago, punished his boy. That boy would have

needed the punishment if he had been guilty as charged. The father was sure of his guilt. After the punishment was administered, however, the father found that his boy was innocent. But instead of going to him and apologizing, he said, "What I have written I have written," with the result that a black scar remains on that boy's life to this hour. Many a home is today in ruins, in spite of the fact that husband and wife still love each other. But the chasm that separates them will never be bridged because they are too stubborn to apologize.

This same attitude of stubbornness has wrecked many a fine friendship. Perhaps your friend did you a wrong. Or, what is harder still to forgive, you may have wronged him. Since then you have stubbornly avoided each other while love has been slowly changing into hate. Such a course does nothing but harm. When I was a boy I had a very painful stone bruise. I found no relief till it was lanced and the inner corruption discharged. An apology often lets the inner corruption out of our hearts. It is a blessing to the one who is wronged, but it is a far greater blessing to him who did the wrong. But failing to apologize, we often lose our friend and work untold harm to ourselves.

If our stubborn refusal to confess that we are wrong makes impossible our receiving the forgiveness of a friend, it also makes impossible our receiving the forgiveness of God. It was just such refusal on the part of Pilate that worked his undoing. He had written a tragic and bloody record. But in spite of that fact, if he had only dared to confess, God would have forgiven him. But with the obstinate declaration, "What I have written I have written," upon his lips, he went out into the night. Some have pictured him in the afterdays as washing his guilty hands in an agony of remorse. But Anatole France comes closer to the truth. He pictures him in a yet hotter hell. He tells us that one day when Pilate was living in retirement a friend called to see him. In the course of their conversation this friend asks this question, "Pilate, do you remember that young Jewish Rabbi that you sentenced to death when you were Governor in Jerusalem? His name was Jesus of Nazareth." In answer, Pilate knits his brows and murmurs thoughtfully, "Jesus of Nazareth—No, I don't remember him." There could be no sadder tragedy than that.

But you and I have a stake in this story. How about your record and mine? "What I have written I have written" is a word that befits the lips of all of us. Our records are not altogether bad, thank God. But neither are they altogether good. Since this is the case, why not confess it before our Lord who is so eager to forgive? Why not defy our stubbornness and pray the prayer of the Publican, "God be merciful unto me a sinner"? This proved for him an open door to life. It will do the same for ourselves. And mark you, there is no other door. "If we say that we have no sin, we deceive ourselves, and the truth is not in us. If we confess our sins, he is faithful and just to forgive us our sins, and to cleanse us from all unrighteousness." This is our gospel. It fits into our needs because it is a gospel for sinners. May God give us the grace to receive it.

XI

HEARTLESS LIARS

"It is your affair, not ours."

MATTHEW 27:4 (Moffatt)

"IT IS YOUR AFFAIR, NOT OURS." HOW FAMILIAR ARE these words! They are as fresh and up-to-date as our last alibi. Yet, they are as old as sin. We have all uttered them at one time or another. They are as abiding as human hate and selfishness. Of all the cruel words uttered in connection with the crucifixion of our Lord, none are more cruel than these. They are as fiendish as they are false. Such lies are doubly deadly. They are destructive to those who utter them. They are likewise destructive to those to whom they are spoken.

You will recognize these words as part of the tragic
story of Judas' betrayal of his Lord. For mingled
motives of greed and jealousy and hate he flung the Man
he once called Master to his enemies. But now that the
deed is done a terrible reaction has set in. A thousand
beautiful memories plead, "like angels, trumpet-tongued,
against the deep damnation of his taking-off." The
petty reward for this deed seems to bite like a serpent
and sting like an adder. Thus tortured, Judas hurries
back to those who shared in his crime, to the men who
had duped him. He feels that if he throws away the
money, he will thus fling away some bit of his guilt.
"I have sinned," he sobs, "in that I have betrayed
innocent blood." But what answer do these religious
leaders give to this desperate man? They answer with
this heartless lie: "It is your affair, not ours."

I

Now in calling these cruel words a lie, we do not
mean that there is no bit of truth in them. There are
few lies that are Simon-pure. A lie needs a coating of
truth in order to be effective. This declaration of the
priests has a real truth in it. No man would be quicker
to confess this than Judas himself. What is there true
in this hellish word? This: "It is your affair." The
treachery of Judas was his own affair. The ghastly
guilt of it was terribly personal. Sin is always a fear-
fully individual matter.

This is the case, in the first place, because the burden

of choice rests upon us as individuals. Judas did not have to betray his Master. He was under no compulsion. I have reminded you of this astonishing and shocking word from one of the greatest of our modern preachers: "I do not believe that Judas was a man in the ordinary sense of the word. I believe that he was a devil incarnate, created in history for the nefarious work which was hell's work." But for us this is unbelievable! If this minister is correct, then Judas was not responsible for the betrayal of Jesus any more than I would be responsible if I were forced to play the part of Iago. If Judas were created to play the part of traitor, then he merely fulfilled his destiny, and is in no sense to blame.

But Judas was not a monster; he was a man. He was made of the same material of which you and I are made. He was free to make his own choice, even as you and I. Before he came to this tragic choice he had made smaller choices that were wrong. Having been unfaithful to the day-to-day demands that were placed upon him, when he came to this bigger test he was guilty of this glaring infidelity. This big failure was in a sense the sum-total of the smaller failures of his yesterdays. And the resulting guilt was his very own. This is ever the case when we make wrong choices. We are accustomed to speak of "my house, my money, my land," but these are only possessions. They are not really ours. Other hands have fingered them before we came upon the scene. Other hands still will finger them when we behind the vale have passed. But our guilt is our very own. "My sin," sobs the Psalmist, with true spiritual insight, "is ever before me." Judas was as lonely in his guilt as if he were the only man that had ever sinned.

Here is a story to the point. Some years ago in a certain community a man committed a ghastly crime. There then followed a horrid event that left a blacker blot on that community than the original outrage. A mob gathered, took the law into their hands, and brutally executed the accused. There was one man, I am told, who joined in the murder that could not get the crime off his conscience. It tortured him. It was vain for him to remind himself that more than a hundred others took part in the lawless deed. It was vain for him to try to divide the guilt by the number that were engaged in the crime. He could not but feel that the affair was his very own. He realized that he was as guilty as if no hand had had a part in the deed except his blood-stained hand. Goaded by this conviction, he at last took the way of Judas and flung himself out of the world.

It was the keen, ambitious mind of Lady Macbeth that gave birth to the plan for the murder of Duncan. She was hard and ruthless, far beyond her husband. In fact, she knew that it would require much urging on her part to induce him to consent to the crime. "Thou wouldst be great; art not without ambition. . . . . Yet do I fear thy nature. It is too full o' the milk of

142

human kindness to catch the nearest way." She could have done the deed herself. But, heartless as she was, her hand faltered when she saw how like the sleeping Duncan was to her father. It was Macbeth that struck the fatal blow. Thus they became partners in the crime. But they did not share in the guilt in such fashion that each was half a murderer. On the contrary, they were both one hundred per cent guilty. Our sin, however great the multitude with which we share it, is our very own. When, therefore, these priests tell Judas "It is your affair," he knows that they are speaking sober truth.

II

But if there is truth in their statement, there is also in it a fearful lie. Wherein is their answer false? The falsehood is in those two little words, "not ours." When they assert the guilt of Judas, they are simply affirming what Judas already knows. "How do you plead?" we ask this broken man. "Guilty," comes the answer. But the guilt of Judas does not cancel the guilt of these priests. When they say "It is your affair, not ours," they are telling Judas and themselves and the whole world that they have no stake in the affair whatsoever. They are trying to shrug the whole ghastly business from off their shoulders and stand forth totally untouched and unconcerned. But this is impossible. They have a stake in this betrayal whether they ever dare to face and acknowledge the fact or not.

1. This is the case because they and Judas are in the same family. They are a part of each other. "God hath made of one blood all nations to dwell upon the face of the earth." There is such a thing as the solidarity of the race, however we may seek to ignore it. We are a part of each other. Sometime ago a young girl was threatening to marry into a family that was highly objectionable. When this fact was pointed out, she replied with conviction, "I am not marrying the family. I am only marrying John." But there she was mistaken. This she will find when her mother-in-law comes to spend the winter with her. This she will find when her children show traits of the lawlessness that has characterized the family into which she is marrying.

There are certain congressmen that we are accustomed to call "isolationists." They seem to believe that America can withdraw from the world of which she is a part, and live within and for herself. As we witness the tragic plight of the nations of Europe and Asia today we find ourselves wishing that this could be the case. But it is impossible. However superior we may feel to those nations that are seeking to destroy each other, we are part of them simply because we are a part of this world. That has always been the case. It is so in a peculiar sense now because our world is getting smaller all the while. We have a stake in the tragedy of others because we are part of them.

2. These priests had a stake in the deed of Judas

because, being of the same family, what hurt him could not but hurt themselves. We have a blind and foolish way of saying, "I have a right to live my own life. What I do is no business of yours." But that is utterly false. What I do is your business because it either helps or hurts you. What you do is also my business for the same reason. We are bound in a bundle of life with each other. Your faithfulness helps me to be faithful. Your moral failure helps me to fail. "No man liveth to himself."

Take the matter of liquor drinking, for instance. If I want to take a drink, whose business is it? Well, it is the business of those who have to live with me. Not only so, but it is the business of others more remote. It is the business of those who travel the same streets and the same highways that I travel. When I drink, my reactions are slowed down; my intelligence is blunted; my recklessness is increased. I thus become a danger to myself, but I also become a danger to you. I cannot, therefore, fail to mind my own business without failing to mind yours as well. These men, therefore, had a stake in the crime of Judas because they were weakened by that crime.

3. Then they had a stake in the crime of Judas because they had helped to make Judas what he was. Some of them had perchance helped passively. They may never have spoken to Judas; but, by being the kind of men they were, they had helped to create an atmosphere in which loyalty was hard and disloyalty

was easy. I think we have never recognized the power for good or ill of an atmosphere. We can create such an atmosphere in our homes that our children will grow into a knowledge of God as naturally as a rosebud blossoms at the kiss of the sun. We can also create an atmosphere where the budding spiritual life of the child will be blighted as by a killing frost. We can create an atmosphere in the church that chills and repels. We can also create an atmosphere so genuinely friendly, so beautifully brotherly, that those who worship with us will say, "Surely God is in this place." Every one of us is either making life easier for somebody or making it harder.

But some of these priests were more than passive participants. They had been active and aggressive. They had offered Judas a reward for his crime. They had responded when he had said, "What will you give me, and I will deliver him unto you?" They had definitely sought to buy Judas and thus make him into a traitor and a murderer. Having succeeded, they shared his guilt. They were as fully and completely guilty as if they, and they alone, had betrayed the Master, and had put him to death. We, too, have a stake in the burdens, the failures, the sins of our fellows. We are a part of them; being thus a part, if one member suffers, all members suffer with it. Not only so; but we are often one with them in guilt, because, either actively or passively, we have helped to make them what they are.

III

But, in spite of this fact, we continue to say with these of the long ago, "It is your affair, not ours." Why do we persist in telling this age-old lie? We are moved by the same motives that actuated these priests. Why did they speak to Judas in this fashion?

1. Because of indifference. When this broken man came to them with the story of his guilt, they were not in the least concerned. Not only so, but they seemed to take a kind of malicious pleasure in informing Judas of that fact. "It is your affair, not ours." What did they mean by this? It was their way of saying, "We are not the least interested in your pathetic plight. It does not matter to us in the slightest whether you live of die, sink or swim." Their declaration was born in part of an icy indifference.

2. Not only was there indifference in this reply, but there was also contempt. Having made a tool of Judas, having bought him and paid for him, they now felt at liberty to throw him away. That happens again and again. We are very prone to regard with contempt those whom we have bent or bribed to our purpose. Years ago I knew a man of means who courted a lovely country girl. She was the only daughter of a widowed mother. By promises of marriage he won her and betrayed her. When, as an expectant mother, she told him of the disgrace that was creeping upon her; when she appealed to him to make good his promise of marriage, his answer was strangely like that of these priests.

"That is your affair," he said, "not mine." Sadder still, those closest to her seemed to take the same position. Naturally there was but one door open to her, and through that dark door she plunged. These priests and scribes spoke in contempt.

3. Along with this contempt there is a note of superiority. "You contemptible traitor," they seem to say. "We have used you, it is true; but we would never have done a deed like that ourselves. We are quite decent and respectable, but you are utterly hopeless. Do not ask us to do anything for you. We would be ashamed to be caught in your company." Thus they looked upon Judas as we who are respectable sinners often look upon those who have gone glaringly wrong— with a sense of superiority. Their plight does not move us to pity. It rather leads us to thank God that we are not like themselves.

4. But the supreme motive back of this assertion, I think, was a desire to save themselves trouble. These men simply did not wish to be bothered. Judas was suffering. Should they take this appeal seriously, they would have to suffer with him. They simply could not afford to get under his load. Not only so, but they did not wish to feel mean and ashamed for having thrown him aside. They rather desired to go their heartless way feeling quite comfortable, and without the slightest pang of conscience. For this reason they told Judas and themselves, "It is your affair, not ours."

There is within all of us an instinctive shrinking

from the cross. What is it to bear the cross? It is voluntarily to take upon ourselves the other man's burden. Too few of us are willing to do this. Let him that is without sin cast a stone at these priests. Personally, the realization of my own selfishness paralyzes my arm. So many times have I said by my deeds, if not by my words, "It is your affair, not ours," so many times have I shirked the cross and refused to make my brother's need my own that I cannot look with utter scorn upon these ancient shirkers. I can only say, "God be merciful to me a sinner."

IV

What was the outcome? Judas came to these religious leaders because he was in desperate need of help. But they greeted him with indifference and contempt. They refused to get under his load with him. How did it work? How does it work today when we take the same attitude? Does this conduct offer us a cue as to the best way to use life or does it not? Suppose we all follow their example, suppose we all stand from under, saying to every needy brother, "It is your affair, not ours," then what? We can find our answer in this story of the long ago. By meeting the appeal of Judas with crass selfishness, they failed to help him. Not only so, but they made him feel that there was nothing left for him but suicide. Their attitude was deadly then, and it is equally deadly today.

If the selfish attitude of these priests worked ruin

to Judas, we may be sure that it was no less ruinous to themselves. We can make the same choice. We can look upon human need, shrug our shoulders, and stand from under. But in so doing we not only miss the high privilege of serving, but we surely destroy ourselves. "He that seeketh to save his life shall lose it." When? Where? Not at some far-off day beyond the grave. We lose it at this very moment and at this very place. To refuse to give is to refuse to live. To follow the cue of these priests is to destroy ourselves and to help destroy our fellows and our world.

Suppose, then, we try Christ's way. Here it is: "Bear ye one another's burdens, and so fulfill the law of Christ." That is the law by which Jesus lived. He was constantly taking the burdens of others upon himself. Every man's need was his need. Every man's pain was his pain. He bled through the wounds and wept through the tears of others. At last in his passion for being helpful he went to the Cross. With what result? He really lived, abundantly, grandly, joyfully. Not only so, but he brought springtime to a frozen and wintry world. If we are to win, his way must become our way.

> "O Cross that liftest up my head,
>   I dare not ask to fly from Thee;
> I lay in dust life's glory dead,
> And from the ground there blossoms red
>   Life that shall endless be."

XII

THE OVERCONFIDENT FRIEND

*"Though all men shall be offended because of thee,
yet will I never be offended."*

MATTHEW 26:33

SIMON IS SURE OF ONLY ONE MAN. HE CANNOT
count upon the lesser members of the group, Thomas, Matthew, and Philip. He cannot count upon his
true and tried friends, James and John, the sons of
thunder. He has been partners with these in the
fishing business. He has braved dangers with them
on the high seas, but he cannot trust them. He cannot
count with full assurance upon Andrew, his brother,
the brave and tender spirit that led him to Christ. He
cannot even be quite sure of the Master. But there is
one upon whom he can rely with absolute confidence.

That man is himself. Therefore he says, "Though all men shall be offended because of thee, yet will I never be offended."

I

What does this tell us about Simon? There are those who affirm that these bold words indicate that Simon is afflicted with an inferiority complex. They contend that he is using this swaggering speech as a smoke-screen behind which to hide his cowardice. Personally, I do not think so. Simon is a man of real courage. He is especially rich in physical courage. He is on the way to becoming a rock of Christlike character. He is deeply devoted to his Master. When he tells us, therefore, that he is ready to go with Jesus, both to prison and to death, he is speaking what he believes to be sober truth. He was never more genuinely sincere in all his life. Instead of having a sense of inferiority, Simon has the opposite. He is sure of himself. This, I think, is his outstanding characteristic.

In saying that Simon is a man of vast self-confidence, we are ascribing to him a characteristic that many admire. We applaud those who are able to stand on their own feet, who ask nobody and no situation any odds. But in spite of this, those of us who are accustomed to read the Bible cannot shut our eyes to the fact that this apparent virtue is not greatly admired by the writers of the Scriptures. In fact, this self-sufficiency, that seems so like a virtue to us, strikes them as a bit of a vice. They warn against it again and again. "Pride goeth before destruction and a haughty spirit before a fall," declares one. "Seest thou a man wise in his own conceit? there is more hope of a fool than of him," says another. And brilliant and gifted Paul says, "Let him that thinketh he standeth take heed lest he fall."

Now I am not affirming that these ancient thinkers are right. We know many things that they did not know. In some respects we have run far past them. Maybe what was a virtue then is a vice now. They thought highly of humility. But we are not so sure that humility is a virtue after all. Of course, it may be of value at church or at prayer meeting. But when the benediction has been pronounced and the service is over and we are ready to go back to confront the kind of world in which our lot is cast, we feel that we had better leave our humility behind and take on some of Simon's self-sufficiency. In other words, does humility match up with the facts of life better than self-assurance does or not? These ancient writers cast their vote in favor of humility and against self-sufficiency.

II

Why do they do this? What is wrong with self-confidence? What does too much self-assurance do for us?

1. It stops our ears and shuts the door of knowledge in our faces. The only one who learns is the one

who does not know. Our parents would like to share their knowledge with us. They have learned something from the experience of living, but often they cannot teach us because we already know. Why should we listen to these dull and backward souls when we forget more while lacing our shoes in the morning than they have ever known? I used to teach school. The most difficult pupil with whom I had to deal was not the one who was a bit wayward, nor the one who was a bit dull. He was the chap who was born educated. How does Mr. Huxley tell us that he learned science? He did not do so by swaggering. He rather tells us that he sat down before the facts as a little child. That is, he learned through humility. It is the humble to whom the door of knowledge stands ajar. It shuts automatically in the face of the self-sufficient. This is true of knowledge in the realm of the visible. It is true equally in the realm of the invisible.

Why did so many of the cultivated religious leaders of that day reject Jesus? It was not because they were bad men. It was not because they were indifferent. They were desperately earnest. It was not because they had no thought or hope of a coming Deliverer. They treasured the promises of the coming Messiah. Some of them were living in expectation of him. But when he came they could not recognize him because of their conceit. Their pride shut their eyes. They knew so much more than this unlettered Peasant from Nazareth that they could see nothing in him. Jesus was thinking of this type of mind when he prayed this rather startling prayer: "I thank thee, Father, Lord of heaven and earth, because thou hast hid these things from the wise and prudent, and hast revealed them unto babes. Even so, Father: for so it seemed good in thy sight." Of course, Jesus is not rejoicing that the truth is hidden from anybody. That for which he is grateful is that the doorway to knowledge is open to the childlike. Babes can learn what philosophers fail to learn because they come in a spirit of humility rather than that of self-confidence.

It was this self-sufficiency that stopped Simon's ears to the warning of Jesus. The Master might have saved him if he had only been willing to listen. But he was sure that he knew himself better than anyone else knew him, even Jesus. Therefore, when his Master tried to tell him something about himself he would not hear. He knew himself, and could therefore be absolutely certain as to what he would do under any given set of circumstances. "I know," he is saying, "how genuinely I love my Master, how deeply loyal I am to him. Knowing this, I also know that, when the test comes, I will stand true. I will face any ordeal with him, whether it be prison or death." That declaration is not unique. We make such about ourselves again and again. But in so doing, we are likely to be as mistaken as was Simon. Few, if any of us, really know ourselves well enough to be sure of our reaction in the face of a trying emergency.

To be convinced of this, it is only necessary to realize how many things we have done that we never thought we would do. Some time ago I talked with a man who had become a bond-slave of drink. He was an intelligent man, he was kindly. He knew what liquor was doing for him. He knew that it was robbing him of his position, that it was undermining his health. He knew it was cheating him both of his friends and of his family. "If a man had told you ten years ago that you would become what you are today, you would not have believed him, would you?" I asked. "If a man had told me ten years ago," he answered sternly, "that I would ever become what I am, I would have killed him." Jesus tried to tell Simon something of himself and of what he would do, but Simon's self-sufficiency stopped his ears. The man who is sure of himself is not teachable.

2. Self-sufficiency also causes us to throw away our opportunities for preparation. The man who is sure of his ability to meet every emergency does not need to prepare himself for that emergency. Here, for instance, is a football team that so far has won every game. Two weeks away is the last game of the season. The coach is trying to prepare for this final ordeal. But his team is indifferent. "What's the use?" they say. "We have won every game." Thus sure of themselves they break the training rules and refuse to practice. Here is a student who is quite certain that the coming examination is going to be a soft snap. For

him to do any reviewing would be only a waste of time. Thus he also is too sure of himself to prepare for the coming test.

3. Overconfidence by thus robbing us of preparation opens the door to failure.

Why did Jesus bring Simon and his two friends with him into the inner precincts of the Garden? It was that there in his fellowship they might prepare themselves for the ordeal that was ahead. Jesus was wise enough to avail himself of this opportunity. Before the soldiers and the mob arrived he prepared himself by earnest prayer for the coming conflict. Simon and his friends refused to make such preparation. Thus refusing, they headed toward disaster. This is the case because we constantly enter the doors for which we are prepared. "They that were ready went into the feast." In the faces of all others, the door is shut. Simon slept when he should have prayed, therefore his testing hour found him fit only for failure. He had enough physical courage to strike one blow. Had the fight been purely of force, Simon might have stood his ground. He might have forgot his fears in the stress of the conflict. But he was unprepared for this kind of fight.

"Put up thy sword into its sheath," said the quiet voice of Jesus. "For he that taketh the sword shall perish by the sword." At that Simon's courage went from him. He dropped his useless weapon to flee into the night. In the dim shadows he pulled himself together, and began once more to follow his Master, who was now under arrest. But the story says that he followed afar off. He did not have the courage to press close to his side. Thus he robbed himself of that intimate fellowship that would have given him strength. Not only so, but he dared to sit down among the servants of the High Priest, and to warm himself by their fire. Thus Simon robbed himself of a bracing atmosphere to put himself into one that was indifferent, if not entirely unfriendly. Thus he headed toward utter collapse. When questioned about his discipleship, he went to pieces. He denied that he had ever known Jesus. Seeing that his palpable lie was detected, he tried to prop it up with oaths. Then the cock crowed, and Peter remembered, and the horror of his disloyalty rolled over him like a flood. But he had only entered the door for which his neglect of preparation had made him ready.

Now we miss the whole point of the story if we fail to realize that Simon's tragedy is not unique. It is sober truth that "pride goeth before destruction, and a haughty spirit before a fall." That matches up with life. One day my brother and I spent hours catching an ugly and vastly unpromising yearling. We got a rope around the horns of this pitiful looking runt. Then we called a colored playmate, whose name was Nim, and challenged him to ride the beast. Nim looked at the wretched little creature with vast contempt. "What," he said, "do you think I can't ride that little

old thing? Why, I will mash him to the ground.'
"All right," we answered, "get at it." Now my
brother's part was to let loose the rope at the proper
time, while my part was to crank him. We carried out
the program, and it ended for Nim in disaster. As he
picked himself up out of the mud he remarked, "If I
had knowed he had that much strength in him I would
have stuck a little tighter."

Did you ever hear of that frog that wanted to go
south for the winter? He was tired of chilly days
and biting nights. So he decided to make his way
to the land of summer. He asked help of two wild
geese who were friends of his. They agreed to take
him if he could suggest a means of transportation. The
frog was wise, so he secured a good string, instructed
the geese to take each end in their beaks while he with
his mouth layed hold of the middle. Soon they were
in the air, headed toward spring. All went well till
a farmer looked up, saw the unusual sight, and shouted:
"Who invented that?" That was too much for the
frog. "I invented that," he answered, and thus let
go the string, and a moment later the farmer had a
bit of minced frog at his feet.

If this is true in the ordinary affairs of life, it is
equally true in the realm of religion. To reckon without God is to head for disaster. The Bible seems to
have been written very largely to convince us of the
truth of this. Here, for instance, is a story coming
out of a distant past. "By faith the Israelites passed

through the Red Sea as by dry land: which the Egyptians assaying to do were drowned." That is, a horde of slaves who reckoned with God were able to accomplish what a highly organized army could not accomplish whose faith was only in themselves. If that seems too far in the past to be either interesting or convincing, let us make it a little more modern. "By faith the Puritans won the victory: which the Cavaliers assaying to do were defeated." Why the difference? Were the Puritans by nature braver than the Cavaliers? Were they more skillful and more intelligent? By no means. The difference is in this: The Cavaliers trusted in themselves while the Puritans were humble enough to trust in God.

Here is another old story. It is a story in which strength is pitted against weakness; splendid equipment against meager equipment; maturity against youth. But listen to youth! "Thou comest to me with a sword, and with a spear, and with a shield. But I am come to thee in the name of the Lord of Hosts." Goliath trusted only in himself. David trusted in God. It was the man of faith that won. If this also seems too far away to be interesting, we can come much nearer. Here is one of the most self-confident men of all time. His name is Napoleon. He won victory after victory till he declared, "God is on the side of the strongest battalions." By this he meant that God was ruled out. He had no hand at all in the making of history. Nothing counted except force. In this faith

Napoleon marched on Russia. For a while all went well. But one day it began to snow. A snowflake is quite a harmless thing. But a multitude of snowflakes decimated Napoleon's army and sent him home in utter defeat.

Later this genius rallied and gathered other armies. Then came Waterloo. Hugo tells us that Napoleon fought with his artillery, that he held it in his hand as a skilled marksman might hold a revolver. But it rained just before Waterloo, so that his artillery bogged down. Then the night before the battle Napoleon ate onions. The onion, as you know, is a sleep-producing vegetable. So Napoleon's keen faculties were not quite so alert as usual the next morning. Then, unmindful of a deep ditch between his own cavalry and that of the enemy, he ordered a charge with the result that much of his cavalry was buried in this ditch. "God does not count," said Napoleon. Then as another has said, "God took a flake of snow, and a drop of rain, and a ditch, and an onion, and defeated him." He chained him to a rock in the sea where the only possession that was left to him was an old pair of military boots that he insisted on having upon his cold feet when he died.

What, shall we say of the millions that today are seeking to be independent of God? What can we say of those nations, vast and strong, that have turned from God to rely solely upon themselves and upon the force of their armies? This we can say of those that have taken such a course in the long-gone past. They are dead. Since this is true we may be sure that those that take such a course today are headed for disaster. This is just as certain as that night follows day. It is just as certain as the fact that individuals, groups, and nations reap as they sow. Self-sufficiency therefore is not an asset, but a liability. This is proved by the experience both of the individual and of the group.

III

But in spite of his failure, Simon is one of the most helpful men that we meet upon the pages of the New Testament. This is the case because he dared to begin again. Having fallen utterly, he refused to stay down. How did he come to recover?

The first move in that recovery, as always, was made by our Lord. When Simon had done through cowardice, pretty largely what Judas had done through jealousy and hate, Jesus turned and looked upon him. I wonder what was in that look. Did it speak after this fashion: "I told you so. I knew your self-sufficiency would be your downfall. You have failed me when I needed you most. Now, I will have nothing to do with you"? No, that look did not say that. On the contrary, it spoke to Simon of a love that would not let him go, and of a hope that was sure of his return. Simon turned from those tender eyes with a broken heart.

Not only did Jesus look upon Simon with a love

that shamed him while it gave him hope, but he sent him a special message. "Go tell my disciples," he began the sentence. Then he remembered Simon's failure. He knew that Simon, crushed by grief and shame, would not dare to count himself a disciple any more. Therefore, he amended the sentence and said, "Go tell my disciples and Peter." And under the kiss of that gentle sunrise Simon's frozen heart became a landscape of flowers. He felt himself restored once more to his Master's friendship. In that friendship he increasingly died to his own self-sufficiency. Years later, therefore, when he writes to his fellow-Christians, he commends to them a garment that he has worn ever since his tragic downfall and his wonderful recovery. "Be clothed with humility," he urges; "for God resisteth the proud, and giveth grace to the humble."

This is not mere theory with Simon, it is experience. But why is it true? Why does God give grace to the humble and to these only? Because it is only the humble that is willing to receive. How long then are we to be without God? Just so long as we are content to be without him. Just so long as we are sufficient for ourselves. When we realize that there is salvation in none other, when we realize that it is not by might nor by power, but by his Spirit, then we make it possible for God to do in us and through us what he longs to do. Till we learn this we are headed for defeat. "Except the Lord build the house, they labor in vain that build it. Except the Lord keep the city, the watchman waketh but in vain." But when in despair of our own ability we turn to him, then we can shout with another, "In him who stregthens me, I am able for anything."

XIII

THE TIMID FRIEND

"Joseph of Arimathea, being a disciple of Jesus, but secretly for fear of the Jews."

JOHN 19:38

NOT ALL THE FACES ABOUT THE CROSS WERE SIN-ister and unfriendly. There were some that were full of tenderness and kindness. Among the kind faces was that of Joseph of Arimathea. All the Evangelists take note of this cultured and winsome man. All deal with him in a most complimentary fashion. In fact, they seem to vie with each other in pointing out his merits and in telling how highly he was respected by all who knew him. They are evidently genuinely proud of Joseph.

I

Look at some of the good things they have to say about him.

1. He was a man of wealth. Of course they are aware that money is not of necessity a badge of virtue. The Bible is always sane in its dealing with the matter of money. It never makes a hero out of a man just because he has wealth. No more does it call him a villain because of his possession of wealth. This Book looks upon money as neither moral nor immoral. It is non-moral. It is pent-up power, condensed energy. Whether it does good or harm depends upon how it is used. In the hands of a bad man it may do vast harm. In the hands of a good man it may do vast good. The fact that Joseph was rich means that he had a larger capacity to help or hurt than he would have had had he been poor.

2. Joseph was a man of position. He had both social and political position. He was an aristocrat, a blue-blood. Not only so, but he was a member of the Council. He was a part of the Court before which Jesus was tried. Of course we are aware that position is no more an infallible mark of greatness than is money. Through the centuries little men have often succeeded in winning big positions, but they were not always thereby made big themselves. "Pygmies are pygmies still, though percht on Alps." But while position is not of necessity a mark of worth, it is as in the case of money an instrument of power. Joseph therefore, with

his wealth and position, had an ability to be useful or harmful beyond the ordinary.

3. Joseph was a man of fine character. One of the Evangelists tells us that he was a good and upright man. That is the best that has yet been said. Since he was a good man, we may count on his using his wealth, not as its owner, but as a good steward. Since he was a good man, we may well believe that he used his office, not as an opportunity for graft, but as an opportunity to serve. That was as it should be. It is a major curse in our American life that we so often elect small and crooked men to public office. So often, too, these use their office, not to serve others, but to serve themselves. Joseph was a good and upright man.

4. Joseph was loyal to the finest faith of his people. The great prophets of Israel had sought to lead their fellows to expect the dawning of a better day. In spite of present evils and injustices they had looked toward a time when all these should be done away. They foresaw a day when men should beat their swords into plowshares and learn war no more. They believed a time was coming when justice should flow down as waters and righteousness as a mighty stream. For this better world they hoped, for this better world they worked and prayed. Joseph had come to share their daring and bracing dreams. Therefore with the choicest spirits of the centuries he was daily taking his place upon his watchtower to scan the horizon for the dawn-

ing of a finer tomorrow. He was looking and working for the Kingdom of God.

5. Finally, and best of all, Joseph was a disciple.
One day this man of wealth and position, this man of
character and high expectation, had come face to face
with Jesus. The one was a peasant, the other a patrician; the one was from a carpenter's shop, the other
from a palace. But in spite of the wide chasm that
divided them, when Jesus invited this winsome aristocrat to become his follower, he accepted. He did not
go away as did the Rich Young Ruler and so many
others of his class. On the contrary, he then and there
dared to become a disciple. That fact in itself speaks
volumes to his credit. There were not many of his
rank that dared to enter the school of Christ. The
Evangelists naturally tell the story of this fine patrician
with evident pride and joy.

II

But in spite of all these splendid qualities Joseph
had at least one glaring defect. Though a friend, he
was not quite the kind of friend we should choose for
ourselves or for our Master. Though a disciple, his
discipleship, like that of ourselves, was very faulty.
This was the case because Joseph lacked one fine virtue
which all admire. This virtue is admired by the young
and the old, by the cultured and the uncultured, by the
civilized and the barbarian. Joseph was short on courage. He was too timid to confess the Master openly.

Had he met Jesus alone he would gladly have spoken to him. But had he been among his own aristocratic friends when he met him, he might have passed him by. He was a disciple, but secretly, for fear of the Jews.

That is a rather damning sentence. So much is this the case that some of us are ready to say that Joseph was not a disciple at all. When we remember how sternly Jesus warns against the sin of being ashamed of him and of his words, we are apt to conclude that there is no such creature as a secret disciple. But in so arguing we are wrong. If you say there is no such thing as a secret disciple, I offer Joseph as Exhibit A. Our text plainly declares that he was a disciple. Then, too, Joseph himself indicated as much a little later by his conduct. Not only so, but I imagine we have all met a few secret disciples along the way. We have all known some, I dare say, whose names, though not inscribed on the rolls of any church, were yet written in the Lamb's Book of Life. But while we are sure that secret discipleship is a possibility, we are equally sure that it is very rare. We are sure further that it is a type of discipleship that satisfies neither God nor man. This is true for the following reasons:

1. To be a secret disciple is greatly to increase one's difficulties. It is to be a Christian in the hard way. To be a genuine disciple on any terms involves difficulty. Sometimes in our eagerness to win recruits we fail to face this fact. Jesus never made that mistake. With

captivating frankness he said that to be his follower meant the denial of self and a daily bearing of the cross. When asked as to the number of the saved, he answered, "Strive to enter in." "Strive," that is a strong word. Its muscles are tense and its brow is wet with the sweat of conflict and struggle. To be a Christian at all means battle, but to be a Christian secretly is to make that battle far more difficult.

Of course Joseph did not decide to keep his discipleship secret for this reason. He was not trying to find the hardest way to be a Christian. He was trying to find the easiest. But in spite of his purpose, the way he chose is the hardest of all hard ways. It is easy to see why this is the case. The same is true in so many other relationships. Here, for instance, is a young chap away at school. He has come from a home of comparative poverty. The fact that he is where he is means that he is being lifted upon the toil-worn hands of a self-sacrificing father and mother. But the boys among whom he finds himself have come from homes of wealth. Their parents are able to supply them, not only with the necessities but also with ample luxuries, and that without having to deny themselves at all.

How is this young fellow to meet this difficult situation? He may do so in one of two ways. First, he may pretend that he, too, is from a home of wealth. In that case he will either live beyond his means, spend far more than he ought to spend, or he will live within his means, and thus lay himself open to the charge of being a skinflint. But, there is a far wiser way. If he has the grit he can face the situation openly. He can tell his friends that he simply is not financially able to spend as they spend. In this way he will make poverty light by acknowledging it. He will also save both himself and his parents from needless embarrassment. Not only so, but he will thus win the respect of every man of his group whose respect is worth having.

The same holds true if our young friend happens to be a Christian while his companions are not. Assuming that he is Christian he will naturally possess certain convictions that his fellows do not share. There will be certain pastimes and dissipations in which they engage without scruples that are impossible for him. Not only so, but there will be certain duties that he will feel that he must perform which his friends habitually neglect. Therefore if he decides to keep his loyalty to Christ a secret, he will be constantly embarrassed. When asked to drink, he will not dare to say that it is against his convictions, he will more likely claim that liquor makes him sick or that he has a headache. In case he wishes to read his Bible he must hide. When he wishes to pray he must wait until the lights are out and he is safe in bed. Thus he is kept in a state of constant conflict, often of shame. But if he were to summon up courage to declare himself once for all, he would find his position vastly easier. He would make one victorious fight instead of a continuous and futile fight. In choosing to be a secret disciple, therefore, Joseph chose the hard way.

2. Not only did Joseph increase his difficulties, by choosing to be a secret disciple, he also greatly increased his dangers of failure. The road of secret discipleship is one that is fairly littered by wrecks. For every one who succeeds in this trying conflict, I am sure that thousands fail. The reasons for this are obvious. The best mode of defense is always to attack. Then, too, for me to confess my faith is to gather new strength within myself. It is further to brace my position by the confidence and expectations of my fellows. "I must be true," I say to myself after my open confession. "There are those who trust me, I cannot let them down." But if I have made no open confession it is doubly easy for me to fail. I have only to say to myself, "No one will know, I have not promised anybody anything." Thus countless thousands have renounced their secret loyalty and made shipwreck of their faith.

Then Joseph increased his danger of failure for another reason. When he chose to keep his discipleship a secret he greatly lessened his chances of growth. In fact, he thus set his feet on a path of increasing weakness rather than one of increasing strength. To come face to face with a difficulty and try to dodge it, is to some extent to clip the thews of our strength. We do not grow strong by dodging the hard and forbidding, we rather grow weaker. But when we face the difficulty and overcome it we grow stronger. Do you remember the story of Samson? One day as he was walking a certain road a lion roared out against him. This lion was right in Samson's way. He was blocking traffic. Therefore this ancient hero had to do one of two things. He had either to beat a retreat or to make a fight. He chose the latter course. So they fell to, the young man and the young lion, with the result that Samson won the victory.

That is fine, but the story does not end there. Days later Samson passed that way again. He decided to turn aside to see the lion that he had slain. When he did so, he discovered that a hive of bees had made their nest in the carcass of the slain beast. Thus he came away with his hands full of honey. This is the author's way of telling us that the strength of every foe we meet and overcome has a way of entering into ourselves. Joseph missed all the honey by dodging the lion. Thus he weakened himself and greatly increased his chances of failure.

3. Not only did Joseph greatly increase his difficulties and dangers by being a secret disciple, he greatly decreased his usefulness. He was of some service to his Master, but that service was only a meager fraction of what it might have been. One of the Evangelists, seeking to say the best possible about him, tells us that when Jesus was before the Council and was sentenced to death, Joseph did not concur. Well, that was something. Joseph tried to tell himself that it was enough; but he could not get away with it, not even with him-

self. As he saw Jesus led away to Calvary he told himself over and over that it was not by his vote. But, argue how he would, he knew that to refuse to concur in an evil is not enough. There are silences that are as damning as the loudest of lies.

Suppose Joseph had taken the course that he knew he ought to take. Suppose he had stood up before that hard and fierce court and had spoken his honest convictions. "Gentlemen, you cannot know how difficult it is for me to take the position that I am now taking and to say what I am now going to say. I know your bitter hatred against this young Prophet. I once shared that hatred. But I reached the conclusion that I had no right to condemn him or anyone else without giving a hearing and seeking to know the facts. I gave him a hearing. Having done so, I have found in this Carpenter the same values that I find in God. I have therefore chosen him as my Lord and Master. That I have not openly confessed my faith and loyalty before is my sorrow and shame. But I confess him now, and stand ready, if needs must, to die with him. I can do none other, God help me."

Suppose, I repeat, that Joseph had plucked up courage to stand in the open, there is no measuring the good that such a daring confession might have done. By it he might have prevented the greatest crime of history. By it he might have won many who looked wistfully to Jesus, but did not quite have the courage to cast in their lot with him. But one thing he would surely have done, he would have brought measureless joy to the heart of Jesus. Not only so, but he would doubtless have saved himself some of the hottest tears that ever burned a human face. But Joseph missed this big chance at usefulness because, though a disciple, he dared not come into the open. Therefore, in spite of his many fine qualities, we are disappointed in Joseph.

III

But this good man saw the error of his way and came to confess Christ before the world. "He plucked up courage," says the record, to go to Pilate and ask for the body of Jesus. Everybody in Jerusalem soon knew of Joseph's open confession. I can imagine that this news produced, even at that time, a bit of a sensation. Some said they had suspected it all along. Some were shocked. Some were grieved and angered. The friends of Jesus rejoiced, at least they did so a little later when their Master had risen. But the greatest joy was that of Joseph himself. In the after days he delighted to tell how the Master, whom he had once feared to confess, had forgiven him and had come to trust him as if he had never failed. In the coming years also there doubtless were many who came to congratulate Joseph upon the great service he had been privileged to render the Master in giving him such a beautiful burial.

But Joseph could never hear such congratulations without a stab of pain. True he had given Jesus a lovely tomb; but, yesterday, if he had had the courage, he might have given him a home, an open hand, a more loyal heart. He could never fully forgive himself for the fact that he had to lose his Lord before he appreciated him enough to confess him before the world. His story is very human, very like our own. Often we too must lose before we appreciate. Thus we sometimes send our sweetest flowers to those who can no longer be gladdened by them. We speak our tenderest words into ears that can no longer hear, and to hearts that can no longer grow warm and tender.

We rejoice with Joseph that he became an open disciple. By so doing he found a fuller salvation than he had known before. But we cannot shut our eyes to the fact that he missed much by not coming sooner. Perhaps there are some here who are trying to be Christian after the fashion of Joseph. Maybe you are a father. In your heart you are seeking to be loyal to Christ, but you have never openly confessed Him, even before your own children. Believe me, you are cheating them as well as yourself. Five years from now, ten years perhaps, something may bring you to an open confession. But the fuller salvation that you will find then cannot possibly mean as much as that that is offered to you today. In fact, there will never be another hour in all the eternities that an open confession of your faith in Christ can mean as much to yourself and to others as it will mean if you make it now. The one right way to be a disciple is to be one openly; the right time to be a disciple is the present. Therefore, I close with this old-fashioned word: "Now is the accepted time: today is the day of salvation."

XIV

ANNAS THE POLITICIAN

"To Annas first."

JOHN 18:13

❋

IN LOOKING AT THE FACES ABOUT THE CROSS, WHICH, think you, is the most sinister? On whose shoulders above all others rests the responsibility for this supreme crime of history? Whose hands are the most stained by this innocent blood? To assess the exact degree of guilt on the part of anyone who has participated in a crime is not always easy. In such matters it is not always possible to speak with dogmatic certainty. Yet it is my conviction that we can indicate with decided assurance not only the group that was most responsible for the death of Jesus, but the individual in that group. Who was he?

He was not any one of the thoughtless crowd that surged about Jesus, mouthing insults that they only partially understood. This crowd played its part, and that part was ugly enough. It was the crowd that, when offered a choice between Jesus the Christ and Jesus Barabbas, shrieked themselves hoarse asking for Barabbas. It was the crowd that, when Pilate, fighting for his own life and that of his Prisoner, had said, "I am innocent of the blood of this righteous man," had shouted back, "His blood be upon us, and upon our children." Their guilt was awful, but any thoughtful reading of the story will show that these were not instigators of the crime. They were but pawns pushed about by the cunning and bloody hands of others.

Pilate also played a shameful part in the death of Jesus. It is hard to exaggerate his guilt. We remind ourselves of his ghastly crime every time we recite our creed. He was set to deal out justice, but dealt out the opposite. His duty was to defend the innocent and to punish the guilty, but he reversed the order and let the guilty go free while he sent the Innocent to his death. More horrible still, he did this not from ignorance, but with eyes wide open. He did it against his own strong and clear convictions. He did it because he was a mixture of rascal and coward. There is therefore no mistaking the damning guilt of Pilate. Yet his is not the supreme guilt. Jesus said as much himself. "He that has delivered me unto you," he said to Pilate. "is more guilty than you are."

The supremely guilty man then was not this weak governor who struck his flag to the god of noise. This stained man was somebody behind the scenes who put Jesus into the governor's hands. Who was that man? "Judas," many answer at once. But in so saying I am sure that they are mistaken. Judas alone could never have delivered Jesus to Pilate. This is, of course, no denial of Judas' guilt. We recognize the fact that he played a most hideous and despicable part. It was so terrible that he himself could not endure the stark horror of it. In bitter remorse he threw away the reward of his treachery and then threw himself away. Judas was so guilty that his Master said of him, "Good were it for that man had he never been born." But even then he does not hold first place. He betrayed his Lord with a kiss, put an abiding curse upon a once good name, and then flung out into the night. Yet guilty as he is, there is another, in my opinion, that is more guilty than he.

Who, I repeat, is this man? There is no question as to the most guilty group. It was the High Priests and their crowd. But who was the prime mover among these? I am convinced that it was none other than Annas. It was he that had Jesus arrested on that Thursday night. It was to his house that he had Him brought. It was Annas before whom He was first tried. It was this crafty priest that delivered Jesus to Pilate. I believe that we can catch a glimpse of the manipulation of his skilled hand in every part of the tragedy. I have an idea that it was Annas who bribed Judas. It was shrewd Annas who gave instructions as to how to manage the mob. It is my opinion that it was Annas who cowed and bullied Pilate. Possibly it was this skilled plotter who had shouted that fateful word, "If thou let this Man go, thou art not Caesar's friend." Therefore as we look into the sinister face of Annas we see, I am sure, the man who, above all others, brought about the death of Jesus.

II

Who was Annas? He was a shrewd and highly successful politician. I here use the word politician in its worst sense. A politician is a man whose supreme passion is to win and hold office. He is willing to pay any price in order to be elected. Once in power, his one question is how he can stay there. The politician may believe very strongly in his fitness for his place and in his superb capacities to serve his people. But his prime purpose in seeking office is not to serve his fellows, but to serve himself. In the open he is a self-forgetful friend of the people. Behind the scenes he is a friend only to himself and to his henchmen. He has two major passions, love of power and love of graft. Such a politician was Annas.

This shrewd schemer was at this time seventy years of age. We resent him all the more for that reason. We feel that, having lived so long and having come so close to the sunset, he should have learned some real wisdom. But the passing years have taught him nothing of life's finer values. Though he has already seized with his grasping hands far more than he can hold, he seems more greedy than ever. Though tottering under the weight of years, he is more bent on getting his while the getting is good than ever before. He is thus an evil old man into whose crafty face we cannot look without a shudder. But of course he has not always been like this. Once he was a youth of marked ability. Probably he was reared in a pious home, under the influence of a good father and mother. He had at one time perhaps been genuinely interested in religion. But, interested or not, he had entered the service of his Church and had become High Priest. Maybe he won this important office through merit, maybe by baser means. Be that as it may, he came both by virtue of what he was and by virtue of his position to be a man of great power.

How did he use this power? He used it to graft and to win more power. Perhaps he found success such heady wine that it intoxicated him. Perhaps he found power and its rewards such a powerful narcotic that he felt he must drink to the full. Anyway he fell under the suspicion of Rome and was dismissed from office. Then what? He did what shrewd and rascally politicians have been doing through the centuries. He ruled from behind the scenes. Years ago my state voted dry. But the mayor of its leading city refused to close the saloons of that city. As a result impeachment proceedings were brought, and he was put out of office. But this was not the end. He built up a machine. This he did by consistently rewarding his friends and by constantly punishing his enemies. To this day he rules with the autocratic powers of a Hitler, and there seems nothing anybody can do about it. Of course his case is not unique. While we take pride in the rule of the majority, we are usually ruled by well-organized minorities, and too often by crooked minorities at that.

Here is how Annas worked it. He had five sons. He made them High Priests one by one. When Annas had gone the rounds with his sons he then chose his son-in-law, Caiaphas. But how had this impeached man been able to put one of his own choosing into office year after year? We can only guess the answer to that question. Since he was so up-to-date, my guess is that sometimes he bullied, sometimes he bribed. Given sufficient funds, there are few offices that a politician cannot win. That was so yesterday; it is so today.

But how had Annas come to possess so much money, for he was vastly rich. Through being High Priest for a time in fact, then through controlling that office from behind the scene, he had been able to get the revenues of the temple very largely into his own hands. When worshipers came to offer sacrifice, they had to have doves or animals to offer. He had a monopoly on selling doves and animals for sacrifice. When Jews from other lands came to worship and to pay their dues they had to change their money into the coin of the realm. Annas also had the money-changing privileges in his power and could charge for exchange pretty largely what he pleased. Thus Annas the politician had managed to win and to cling to power by trickery and by graft.

It is evident from this that Annas was a very modern man. He would be quite as much at home in many American cities today as he was in Jerusalem. He may have had something good about him. I am sure that he did. But I have not been able to find it. He was a part of a conquered people. Rome had its Germanic foot upon the neck of his nation. But, while honest patriots burned with indignation at this, it worried Annas not at all. In fact, he was on the best of terms with the conquerors. He would not have turned the tables on them if it had been in his power. This was the case because, under their protection, he could graft and plunder his fellows in safety. He was a fifth columnist. He was grasping and greedy, treacherous and cruel. In fact, I can think of no other man in all the Bible who was so completely devilish.

III

But why was Annas so eager to destroy Jesus? It was because he saw in Jesus a threat to himself and to his interests. It was in the nature of things that Jesus and Annas should clash. They could no more get along together than light can get along with darkness. Annas was shrewd enough to know that the reign of such rascals as himself is made possible, as a rule, by the indifference and cowardice of the good and the itching palms of the bad. There are always those who say indignantly, "Something ought to be done about Annas." "Why, then, do you not do something?" I ask. "I am afraid it will hurt my business," answers one. "I am too busy," is the reply of another. These cannot even take time to vote. Meanwhile the brotherhood of the itching palms bestir themselves and keep Annas in office. But Jesus was neither greedy, indifferent, nor afraid. But why did not this powerful aristocrat ignore this penniless Peasant? That is just what he and his crowd tried to do. They were eager to destroy Jesus by the thunders of silence, but they could not. This bold Young Prophet continued to be both a rebuke and a threat.

Jesus rebuked Annas in a twofold fashion. First, he rebuked him by being the kind of man that he was. Both Jesus and Annas were religious men. Both claimed to be servants of the people. But even the blind could not fail to see the wide chasm that divided them. Jesus declared both by word and deed that he had not come to be ministered unto, but to minister. But Annas had come for an opposite reason. He was not bent on giving, he was bent only on getting. Against the white background of the personality of Jesus men could not fail to see something of the ugliness of this politician. Annas was unpopular at best, but Jesus could not fail to increase that unpopularity. This angered Annas and filled him with envy. This shrewd politician therefore made up his mind that this popular Preacher must be put out of the way. "Pilate knew that for envy they had delivered him."

But Jesus not only rebuked Annas by being what he was, he rebuked him openly by what he said and did. One day the Master went into the temple. There he was horrified by the way in which this temple was being desecrated. The henchmen of Annas were greedily plying their trade. The sight filled the Master with hot indignation. He seized a scourge of cord and drove these traders and money-changers out of that sacred place. "Take these things hence," he said with compelling authority. "It is written, My Father's house shall be called a house of prayer for all nations, but you have made it a robbers' cave." Who were the leaders of these brigands? Annas and his family. But the prize crook, the man higher up, the big boss of the gang, was none other than Annas himself. That, every intelligent man knew. But nobody had ever dared to affront and defy this powerful politician like that before. Something had to be done about it, or the reputation of Annas would soon be torn into even smaller shreds than it was already.

But the supreme offense of Jesus was not against the reputation of Annas. This old rascal did not have much of that to lose. His big offense was that He was a threat to the privileges that Annas was enjoying. It is a human trait that men are seldom willing to surrender a privilege. This is generally the case regardless of how they came by that privilege. It is usually the case regardless of the danger that might be involved in that privilege both to themselves and to others. Because Annas had been in power, and had lived on graft for so many years, he thought he had a perfect right to go on doing so. In fact, he was so fully convinced of this that he would brook no opposition. When Jesus dared to oppose him He thereby signed his own death warrant.

IV

What was the outcome? That which every sane man in Jerusalem expected. Annas won by a big majority. He knew just the wires to pull. Therefore, he sent Jesus to the Cross with consummate ease. This done, he dusted off his hands and went back to his palace and to his rich revenues feeling quite pleased with himself. It was all so easy that Annas could not repress a chuckle. How absurd that one so weak and with such little backing as that of this Young Prophet should presume to oppose him! I can imagine that Annas actually laughed over it. He was just the kind of man that we would expect to laugh at that which would have made a good man shudder. But by this easy victory he has planted his foot the more firmly on the road to disaster. This is the case because, having chalked up another victory, he is now more convinced than ever that he is clever enough to reverse the laws of nature and gather grapes of thorns and figs of thistles.

Thus, though Annas seemed to have won this battle, he did not thereby win the war. A few days later Death took him in his ruthless hands and wrung him out like a wet rag. But all that Death got for his pains was a few pennies. Annas' real wealth had been squandered long ago. Where Annas went after the experience of death, we do not know. But of this we may be sure, when last seen he was in hell. He was in a hell that was so dark that when he met Incarnate Goodness he failed to see anything in him except something to arouse his antagonism and bitter hate. His hell was so black that he could murder the Prince of Life, then go down to his house feeling that he had done service to both God and man. Surely there can be no deeper damnation than that.

But the curse of Annas was not confined to himself. Annas was bound in a bundle of life with others, even as you and I. Had he taken the road that leads into the heights, he would not have gone alone. Some needy soul would have followed him. Neither did he go alone when he tracked his way into the depths. He was a man of great influence. He could have done much, especially for the group of which he was a part. But he used all his vast gifts to blind, to blight, and to destroy. Seeking to serve himself, he missed all the treasure that was real and ended by crashing into ruins like a giant of the forest. But sadder than his own fall was the fact that, like the giant of the forest, he flung out his arms and gripped countless lesser trees and carried them down with him.

The blight that Annas put upon his intimates, he also put to some extent upon his whole nation. By what he was and by what he did he helped to make religion ugly and hateful. He thus helped to undermine character, to destroy patriotism, to blast the very fundamental integrities by which the soul and by which the nation live. For that which makes a nation strong is the character of its people. However wide its boundaries, however numerous its population, however strong its military defenses, if its citizenry is unscrupulous and self-seeking it has within itself the germs of desolation and death. There is no deadlier foe to all that we hold dear than politicians of the types of Annas.

On the other hand, the greatest service we can render to our nation and to ourselves is by being the right kind of men and women. You remember what Elisha said when Elijah was on his way home? "My father, my father!" he cried, "the chariot of Israel, and the horsemen thereof." "There," he declares, "goes the real defender of our nation. You thought Israel's army wore a uniform, but in reality it has been wearing a prophet's mantle." That is simply to say over again what we have tried to say so many times. The one safeguard of a nation is honest, clean, public-spirited, Christlike men and women. By degenerating into a politician Annas became a menace both to himself and to others. Let him that is without some bit of that same sin cast the first stone at this public enemy of long ago.

XV

THAT FOX

"Go ye, and tell that fox, Behold, I cast out devils, and I do cures today and tomorrow, and the third day I shall be perfected."

LUKE 13:32

❧

THERE IS A QUIET MAJESTY ABOUT THAT SENTENCE. The Pharisees have come to tell Jesus that he must leave the country because Herod is seeking to kill him. Of course, these Pharisees are not bringing this information because of their friendship to the Master. They are rather seeking to drive him to Jerusalem, where they are going to kill him themselves. But Jesus answers with quiet dignity and assurance, "I am going on about my God-appointed task in spite of what you or Herod may do. I am going to bring this task to completion through my death at Jerusalem." This text

throws a strong light on Jesus' consciousness of his
mission. It also tells us that his death was not simply
a tragic accident, but that it was the very climax of
his achievement. It was only through his death that
he could utter that tremendous word that he uttered
on the cross: "It is finished."

But our present interest in this text is not because
of the light that it throws upon Jesus, but upon Herod
Antipas. "Go ye, and tell that fox," said Jesus. The
Master sometimes rebuked and rebuked very sharply,
but he was not accustomed to single out one individual
and brand him with an ugly name. But here he calls
Herod "that fox." That is startling. No other man
ever had so high regard for human personality as did
Jesus. He believed in man as man with a faith that
nothing could kill. He had a deep reverence for human
worth. But here the most reverential and the most
loving of all men could find no better name for one of
his fellows than "that fox." This word is a window
through which we look into the very soul of Herod.

I

What does it tell us about him? What kind of
creature is the fox? To us this beast is not greatly re-
pellant. His name does not fill us with horror and
make our blood run cold. But the fact that this is the
case is not the fault of the fox. The only reason we
regard him as a source of amusement in the chase or
as a furnisher of fur for ourselves instead of as a

dreaded public enemy is because of his physical weakness rather than the possession on his part of any uprightness of character. The fox is a beast of prey. He lives off the bodies of others. He takes without giving. He is cruel, cunning, and heartless. When, therefore, the Master called Herod a fox he was calling him a most ugly name. He was describing a man who at heart was little better than a beast of prey.

Not only is the fox a beast of prey, but he is a little beast of prey. Therefore to his cruelty he adds the contemptible vice of pettiness. He substitutes cunning for courage, speed for strength. Had Jesus called Herod a lion we should have thought of him as cruel and strong, bloodthirsty and courageous. But when he calls him a fox we think of him as at once cruel and cowardly. The fox is only a hero in the hencoop. At the bark of the most cowardly dog he takes to his heels. Thus the picture we get of Herod is that of a shy man who is at once cruel, cowardly, weak, and unprincipled.

The fact that Jesus was right in calling him a fox is indicated by a glance at his life. Take one single episode. One day Herod made up his mind to visit his brother, Philip, who was then residing at Rome. He made the journey and was doubtless received by his brother with all courtesy and respect. But though he was bound to Philip and to Philip's wife by ties of blood, though he owed them the loyalty of a guest, these considerations had no influence at all. He was still the same foxy scoundrel that he ever was. Thus he used the privileges accorded him through this visit to make love to, and to have an affair with, his brother's wife. I suppose he found that Herodias alone understood him. At any rate she consented to elope with him and marry him provided he would send his own wife home. This he consented to do. Thus this fox returned to his palace near the shores of the Dead Sea a bit later, having wrecked both his own home and that of his brother.

Having read this story, we do not wonder that Jesus calls Herod a fox. He was a low, cunning, tricky thief. Of course, you may remind me that Herodias was willing to be stolen. Yet, that fact does not excuse Herod. It is rather strange how often in such matters we decide that an opportunity to play false gives us the right to do so. We do not take the same attitude with regard to lesser values. Take money, for instance. If I were to say to you, "I was down at the bank recently and the cashier left a ten-dollar bill within easy reach of my hand. I seized it at once and slipped it into my pocket. I would consider myself foolish to pass up a chance like that." You would not congratulate me. You would look upon me as a thief. A far greater thief is the man that steals in the moral realm, whatever may be the circumstances. You can see, therefore, the wisdom of the name that Jesus gives to Herod.

II

But while Herod was an evil and corrupt man, he was not altogether evil. That is always the case. No man is ever wholly good, and no man is ever wholly bad. Cunning, cruel, and unprincipled as was Herod, he had a better side to his nature. Among the noxious weeds that grew in the garden of his heart there were still a few flowers. These were sickly and weak and much in need of the sun. But in spite of this they were there making a pathetic effort to grow. Something of this lingering goodness comes out in his relationship to John the Baptist. This great and good man interested Herod immensely, made a tremendous appeal to him, stirred him at times to the depths of his shallow soul.

Just how these two extremes came to meet we cannot say. We are naturally a bit surprised to find foxy Herod occupying a pew in the church of which stern and gallant-hearted John the Baptist is pastor. I can imagine that curiosity played its part in bringing these two together. When John began his ministry in the wilderness he created a great stir. He fairly emptied the villages and cities round about to fill the silent solitudes along the banks of the Jordan with multitudes of eager listeners. He preached a rather stern and harsh gospel, but he did it with such fiery conviction that all sorts and conditions of men flocked to hear him.

By and by rumors of the preaching of this great prophet reached the ears of Herod. He became curious to see him. In spite of the fact that he had given rein to every lust, he was a bit bored. Maybe this strange man would bring him a new thrill. Then, maybe Herod was heart-hungry. Maybe even in his petty soul there was a lingering longing for a better life. Why not give him credit for this? Hunger for goodness and for God belongs not to the saints alone, but to the sinners as well. Such hunger is universal. Others just as bad as Herod have felt such longings. Yes, and have had them satisfied too. Maybe Herod had a sly, unconfessed yearning for help. But whether from curiosity or heart-hunger, or both, these two, John and Herod, one day faced each other. I have an idea Herod invited John to his palace. He did not wish to join the rabble to listen to the prophet. Therefore he arranged for himself and his paramour to hear John alone.

It was a great hour for these two pampered sinners when they stood face to face with this wilderness preacher. It was an hour that might have changed and remade them. It was also an hour of testing for John himself. How did John meet it? He met it with the fine sincerity and courage that had characterized him as a wilderness preacher. Here he did not rebuke the sins of society in general. He came to grips with the ugly cancer that was gnawing at the vitals of Herod and Herodias. It takes no great courage, generally speaking, to preach plainly to a multitude. But to deal faithfully with those who have power to make or to break you, that requires courage of the highest type. That is what John did. He passed for the present over the other nine commandments and dealt with the seventh, the sin of adultery. This man was living with a woman who was not his wife, and this woman was living with a man who was not her husband. John made them face that fact.

Not only so, but he made his rebuke in the most courageous fashion. He might have softened the blow by saying, "You are among a fanatically religious people. They believe strongly in the sacredness of the marriage tie. For you two to disregard it is bad politics. Your conduct, therefore, is not expedient. You would be more popular, you would have less trouble with your subjects, if you would have more regard for their convictions." But he based his plea on the bedrock principle of right and wrong. "In living as you are living," he said, "you are sinning against the fundamental rightness of things. It is not lawful for thee to have thy brother's wife." It took courage to say that.

As Herodias listened her keen, cruel eyes opened wide in amazement. Her face became tense and white with anger. She made up her mind then and there that this bold prophet should pay for those words with his life. She did not get angry with the disease from which she was dying. Instead she only got angry at the physician. But Herod with all his baseness was not quite that low. He, too, listened with amazed resentment. The sermon perhaps made him for a brief period very uncomfortable. Its plain bluntness shocked him. But in spite of this, there was that in the sermon that made a tremendous appeal. The story says that Herod heard John gladly.

That fact takes us by surprise. Few of us like to be told plainly of our own sins. But Herod seems to be an exception. Why was this the case? I think Herod got a bit of a thrill out of meeting somebody that was brave enough to tell him the truth. He had been fawned upon and flattered all his life. His friends had lied to him openly and to the point of nausea. Here at last was one that looked him in the eye and told him the ugly truth about himself. Naturally it shocked him, yet he could not bring himself whole-heartedly to resent it. It was something new to face the facts about himself, even though it made him uncomfortable. It was something new also to face a man good enough, big enough, and brave enough to tell him the truth, even though he might have to pay for such truth-telling with his life. But, be the reasons what they may, the sluggish soul of Herod was thrilled by John and by his preaching.

But Herod did more than thrill at the message of John. He took that message seriously. Under John's preaching, Herod's conscience, after suffering long from sleeping sickness, began to awake. He determined to make some improvements in his rotten life. The story says that he did many things. He doubtless vowed that he would leave off some of his evil practices. At least one of the many things that he did was to resolve that he would not be so quick to shed innocent blood. Hence he began by protecting the life of the prophet who had rebuked him. Herodias was for putting John to death then and there. But Herod would not stand for it. There were still some crimes that even this cruel fox refused to commit.

But though Herod did many things under the preaching of John, he did not do the supreme thing. That was his tragedy. He spent his time tampering with the outside of his life instead of having it set right at the center. He saw that his clock was not running right. Therefore he sought to polish the hands. But he did nothing for the inside. A lovely spring on our farm once became so stenchful that even the horses would not drink from it. We found that an animal had died at its very source. No amount of cleaning and cultivation of the environs of that spring would help. The corruption had to be taken out of its heart. Herod was deeply stirred, but he was not stirred enough to repent. This left him ripe for his continued downward course.

III

One of Herod's most fatal steps downward grew out of his birthday celebration. This foxy man was to have a birthday. Now in those primitive days even intelligent people knew of no better way of celebrating a birthday than to throw a wild party. They thought that the prize way to have a good time was for everybody to get drunk. Of course we have learned far better in these enlightened days. But we must remember that we are here dealing with a rather primitive people. Drink was passed in abundance and all the guests were verging on drunkenness. Now Herodias was keeping an eye on the scene. She had a plan for the satisfaction of her lust for revenge. When she saw that Herod was drunk enough to be a bit of a fool she sent her daughter in to perform a salacious dance. This dance appealed to lustful Herod. When she had finished his enthusiasm knew no bounds. He promised the dancer with an oath that he would grant any request she would make, even to the half of his kingdom. Having received that promise, this daughter hurries to her mother, who instructs her as to the request she is to make. "Give me," she said, "the head of John the Baptist in a dish."

That grim request half sobered Herod. Corrupt and drunken fool that he is, he does not wish to commit this crime. But he has taken an oath. He has made a vow. He must keep his word. Is it ever right to lie? Is it ever right to break a vow that we have taken? Certainly. There are some vows that are far more honored in the breach than in the keeping. I once knew a mother whose daughter brought shame upon her home. This mother solemnly vowed that the daughter should never cross the threshold of that home again. She made it in solemn earnestness. For months she kept it. But by and by she broke it. I was there at the breaking of it, and the peace of heaven came back in that mother's face as a result of breaking that horrible promise. Herod should have broken his vow.

But more binding upon him than his vow was the crowd in which he found himself. "For the sake of them that sat with him," says the story, "he commanded it to be given her." We choose our friends and those friends help to make us or break us. You can choose such friends for yourself that life at its best will be far easier for you. You can also choose such friends as to make right living for you next to impossible. I read a letter sometime ago written by a young chap just before he took his own life. "Bad company," he said, "has been my ruin. I ran with the wrong crowd." Herod, feeling bound by his oath and urged on by this cruel crowd, sent an order for the Prophet's execution. A little later Herodias was gloating over the head of John the Baptist, and that at the very table where John might have feasted had he been more a coward and less a hero.

IV

This brings us to the final scene in Herod's life. His awakening by John was to little purpose, for soon he fell asleep again. But even yet his conscience was not entirely dead. Another peasant Preacher was abroad, and the nation was being stirred to its depths. On everybody's lips was the question as to who this new

Prophet was. Some said that he was Elijah, while others said that he was one of the old prophets come back to life. But Herod was sure as to the Prophet's identity. "This," he declared, "is John the Baptist whom I beheaded." There seems hope for Herod even yet. I doubt if he ever acknowledged this crime before. He had probably blamed it on Herodias or on the crowd. But now in the light of these reports about Jesus he stands alone and face to face with his crime. He acknowledges that bloody deed as his very own.

But this awakening on the part of Herod was very brief. Though still interested in Jesus, his interest was born of antagonism rather than of friendliness. Then his antagonism died and he became merely curious. He was still eager to see Jesus, but with no thought of being helped by him. His one hope was that Jesus might give him a momentary thrill by performing some miracle. Herod had his chance at last when the Master was standing under the very shadow of the cross. When the Jews routed Pilate out of bed early that fateful Friday morning and demanded that he try the Master, Pilate did his best to dodge the issue. Learning that Jesus was from Galilee, he hustled him off to Herod. The Fox was gleeful. He began at once to ask Jesus many questions. These questions had been piling up for months. And what answer did Jesus make? He answered never a word, not a single syllable.

That I take it was most startling and amazing.

Why, I wonder, was this the case? It was certainly
not because Jesus was angry at Herod. It was not
because he had lost all patience with him. It was not
because he had ceased to love him. He loves all, good
and bad, with an everlasting love. He did not speak
to Herod because he knew that to speak would do no
good. This fox had trifled with the truth till his ears
had become stopped. He had shut his eyes to the light
till his eyes had gone out. There is sound psychology
in that solemn doctrine of the sin against the Holy
Spirit. It does seem that one may resist the wooings
of the Spirit till he can no longer make his voice heard.
At least the infinitely loving Christ stood in the presence of Herod and had no single word to say to him.

And how did the interview end? Having found
that Jesus would not satisfy his curiosity, in bitter scorn
he threw on him an old purple robe and with loud
laughter sent him back to Pilate. There is something
terrible about that laughter. It sounds as if the hounds
of his own unleashing are closing in upon the Fox.
But we make a great mistake if we convince ourselves
that the case of Herod is unique. However strong
our convictions, we may disregard them till they seem
like mere trifles. However high and precious our
ideals, we may through disloyalty come to scorn them.
There is no deeper tragedy than to reach the place
where we can laugh at those high values that once
brought us with reverence to our knees. H. G. Wells
has a frightful story whose horror grows out of the

fact that the lighted candles in a certain haunted room go out one by one. Maybe that is the tragedy of some of us. One by one our lights are going out. "Let him that thinketh he standeth take heed lest he fall."

XVI

WHEN DEATH IS GAIN

"For me to live is Christ, and to die is gain."

PHILIPPIANS 1:21

❀

THE MAN WHO SAID THIS HAD NOT SEEN THE CROSS literally. But in a most profound sense he had seen it. In fact, he claims that he has been crucified with him who died upon it. He is now writing from a prison cell. Soon he is to stand trial before Nero. He knows, therefore, that in the very near future his prison door is going to open. When it opens he will walk one of two roads. There is the possibility that the verdict will be "Not guilty." In that case the door will open upon the road that leads back to his dearly loved church in the city of Philippi. Set free, he will hurry back to those dear friends of whom he can never think without deepest gratitude. "I thank my God," he says, "upon every remembrance of you." The thought of returning to them and working again with and for them fills him with joy. "I call God to witness how greatly I long after you." Freedom, therefore, will mean the privilege of meeting again with dearly loved friends, and of going on with the work that he loves best, the spreading of the gospel of Christ.

But his prison door may open upon another road. He may be found guilty. In that case there will be a short journey to the place of execution. A few steps and he will lay his head upon the block and the executioner's ax will put a grim period to his earthly life. Thus he is here thinking of death, not as a remote possibility, but as a high probability. Therefore, as he faces these two roads, the one leading to life and work and friends, the other to ghastly death, he is not doing so as one who is merely speculating amidst the safety of the classroom or the cloister. He is rather doing so as one who knows that he is going one way or the other, and that in the immediate future.

I

Now it is interesting to see how Paul faces up to this crisis. He realizes that death is probably very near. He knows of course that ultimately it is an absolute certainty. In what spirit does he face that ugly fact? He does not contemplate death with trembling knees and blanched face. There is no terror in his eyes as he faces the probability of his early passing. No more does he try to ignore the fact of death altogether. That is an attitude that is very common today. There are those that flatly refuse to think of that experience that is ahead of every one of us. They seem to think that they can destroy death by simply refusing to look facts in the face.

But I think we must agree that such an attitude is hardly intelligent. It is a little less than sane. When we say, for instance, that we do not care what lies beyond death we are thinking simply of ourselves. Certainly we cannot say that in the presence of the passing of those we love. Suppose you should visit with me this Easter morning the grave of my mother. Suppose we should stand by that little mound that is now growing green under the miracle of spring. Suppose as we should thus stand I should say to you, "It does not matter to me in the least whether my mother is just a handful of dust today or whether she is consciously alive in the Father's House." Were I to say such a word under those circumstances you would turn from me in horrified amazement. We simply cannot be indifferent about the passing of those we love. There come times, therefore, in all our lives when the biggest of all big questions in this: "If a man die, shall he live again?" Those, therefore, who seek to ignore the fact of death often do so because of fear. But Paul is not afraid.

If Paul does not face the prospect of death with terror, no more does he face it with morbid eagerness. There is something unhealthy about the thinking of the man who is eager to die. He is also afraid. Such a man is afraid of life. It is just as hurtful to be afraid of life as it is to be afraid of death. Paul was not afraid of either. He faced both with calm confidence and joy. "If I am set free," he writes, "it will mean that I will soon be permitted to see my friends again. It will mean that I shall continue to carry on the work that is so dear to my heart. If I am condemned to death, it will mean something better still. Therefore, I hardly know which one to choose. 'For me to live is Christ, and to die is gain.' "

Now, it may be that you do not share Paul's high faith. It may be that you find it impossible to face the future with Paul's calm confidence. If such is the case, to this you must agree: Paul's faith is infinitely worth possessing. To be able to look both life and death in the face, not only without fear, but with a high and joyous expectancy, that is something anybody might covet. Whatever the future may hold for Paul, even if his hopes come to nothing, if all his mad dreams end at last in a handful of dust, his faith is making it possible for him to live grandly and joyously in the here and now. Whether his faith guarantees the future or not, it certainly guarantees the present. He is demonstarting the truth of his own brave words, "Godliness is profitable unto all things, having the promise of the life that now is." He is living grandly now.

II

Why can Paul face both life and death in this joyous and courageous fashion? Why can he look at the grave and say, "To die is gain"?

He cannot do so because such an attitude is inevitable. Death is not always gain. We can easily conceive of circumstances under which death would not be gain, but utter loss. Whether death is gain or not depends upon the values that are possessed by the individual who dies. Suppose all your values are material. Suppose instead of saying, "For me to live is Christ," you say, "For me to live is money." Then to die is not gain. The rich farmer stored all his wealth in barns. When death came it did not enrich him. It left his hands as empty as the pockets of a shroud. If your values are material, the highwayman death will rob you of every one of them.

Suppose you say with Dives, "For me to live is pleasure. For me to live is to be clothed in purple and fine linen and to fare sumptuously every day." If that is all you have, then death will strip you of your purple and rob you of your banquets. Having died, Dives found himself in a situation where all his wealth was not sufficient to buy a single drop of water. If your philosophy is, "Every fellow for himself and the devil take the hindmost," then death will not be gain for you.

It will simply leave you on your own. I can think of no worse hell than to have to look after myself throughout eternity.

For whom then is death gain? Only for those to whom life means what it means to Paul. That is just plain common sense. Death has no power to touch character. Death cannot even change a mathematical formula. Two times two make four. That was true millons of years ago; it will be true throughout eternity. If you have found in the here and now values that really enrich life, you may depend upon keeping those values beyond death. Life is really like the garment of our Lord; it is woven of one piece throughout. Many are accustomed to think of death as if it had in it some magical power. They seem to think that the mere act of dying will work some miraculous change in our character. But such is not the case. The sleep of death can no more transform my essential self than ordinary sleep.

If I lie down to sleep at night, kind and thoughtful of others, if I lie down in the fellowship of my Lord, the mere act of sleeping is not going to break that fellowship. If, on the other hand, I go to sleep harsh and full of hate, and out of touch with my Lord, the mere act of sleeping is not going to bring me in touch with him. If the grave had any power to make a grasping, selfish, evil man into a good man, it might also have the power of making an unselfish and beautiful soul into one that was bad. But death has no such magic. Values that really count here will count throughout eternity. It is, therefore, only those who can say, "For me to live is Christ," that can add that final word, "To die is gain."

III

What did Paul mean by this declaration, "For me to live is Christ"? He meant that there was not a question that one could ask him about himself that he could not answer in terms of Jesus Christ.

1. When he said, "For me to live is Christ," he meant "Christ is the Author of my life. I did not begin in any real sense to live till I met him." Paul is thinking of that experience that he had more than thirty years ago as he journeyed from Jerusalem to Damascus. He was on his way to punish certain Jews whose crime was that they were calling Jesus, Lord. As he journeyed, there burst upon him a vision of the risen Christ. Instantly he was upon his face, saying, "Lord, what wilt thou have me do?" He was doing what he was setting out to punish others for doing, calling Jesus, Lord. As another has said, he had already joined the Church before he reached Damascus. Paul has been an earnest and sincere man up to this hour, but he reckoned that life had really begun for him with this meeting with Christ on this desert road.

It was here that Paul was reborn. It was here that through faith in Christ he came to possess what the New Testament calls eternal life. By eternal life these early saints did not simply mean life that was everlasting in its duration. They were not thinking of a quantity of life, but a quality of life. It was a life that comes only through the knowledge of Jesus Christ. "'He that hath the Son," declares John, "hath life." And Paul speaks of Christ as our life. Both these great Apostles had learned this from the Master himself. "This is life eternal," declares Jesus, "that they might know thee, the only true God, and Jesus Christ whom thou hast sent." "I am the resurrection, and the life." As we find God through Christ we find life eternal, and we find it in no other way.

2. When Paul said, "For me to live is Christ," he meant that for him to live was to reproduce Christ. That is what life is to mean to us in our finite way. We are to reproduce in some fashion the virtues and the sacrificial deeds that made his life the beautiful something that it was. Some years ago a missionary went into a backwoods village in China and began to tell the villagers about Jesus. At once their faces lighted up and their eyes sparkled with understanding. "We know him," they said eagerly. "He used to live here. He is buried in our cemetery." The missionary was filled with amazement. But to prove their declarations they led him to a grave that was kept beautiful by the flowers that loving hands had brought to it day by day. Then they told him of a physician that had given himself, even unto death, to the bearing of the burdens of their needs. And these villagers were right

in saying that in the person of this physician they had a vision of Jesus.

3. Finally, Paul meant by this word that Christ was the aim, the motive, and the goal of his life. He only lived to please Christ. His one purpose and passion was to lay hold of that for which he had been laid hold of by Christ Jesus. To possess Christ and to be like him was the goal of all his hopes and dreams and prayers. "But what things were gain to me, these I counted loss for Christ. Yea, doubtless, and I count all things but loss for the excellency of the knowledge of Christ Jesus my Lord: for whom I have suffered the loss of all things, and do count them but refuse, that I may win Christ." All that life meant to Paul therefore was summed up in Christ. Since this was the case, nothing that either life or death could do could work him ill. For such, all things, here and hereafter, work together for good.

IV

What are some of the gains that Paul expected beyond death?

1. He believed that death would bring him into a more intimate fellowship with Christ. "Having a desire to depart, and to be with Christ; which is far better." He believed that living with him here, he would continue to live with him through eternity. So Jesus taught. Such has been the faith of the saints. Such may be our faith. Be assured that, holding your

hand today, he will not let it go when you come close
to the sunset and evening star. Death will not dim
that face, it will make it only the clearer.

> "Some day the silver cord will break,
>   And I no more as now shall sing;
> But O the joy when I shall wake
>   Within the palace of the King!
> And I shall see Him face to face,
> And tell the story—saved by grace." [1]

2. Not only did Paul believe that death would bring
him into a closer fellowship with his Lord, but also
with the choicest and the best that have lived and died
through all the centuries. Such also may be our faith.
I am interested in the life to come for many reasons.
I am interested because I am acquainted with some that
have passed into that miracle country. I believe that
there are many that I have known that are waiting and
working within the vale. I am expecting the adventure
of death to bring me the finest of all my friendships,
the richest of my associations. I believe that one day
I am going to lock arms with those that "I have loved
long since and lost a while."

3. But Paul was sure that since death would bring
him into a clearer vision of Christ, and to a more intimate fellowship of the saints of all ages, it would bring
him into an atmosphere that is homelike. Jesus thought
of heaven as home. Here are words that have put

---

[1] From "Saved by Grace," by Fanny Crosby. Copyright, Hope
Publishing Co. Used by permission.

their arms round more stooped shoulders and their touch of healing upon more hurt hearts than any other words ever uttered: "Let not your heart be troubled; ye believe in God, believe also in me. In my Father's house are many mansions." Heaven is going to be home. Why? The same characteristics that make home sweet here will make it sweet by and by.

Why is home today the dearest spot in all the world? It does not depend on its surroundings. It does not depend upon the house in which you live. If I were to go back this morning to the home of my childhood, I would find it about the loneliest spot in all the world. Yet the majestic hills that encircled it when I was a boy encircle it still. The trees that fold their green arms about it are once more putting on their Easter loveliness. The Buffalo River still sings its silvery song back of the old farm. The house, though desolate and old, still stands. But it is lonely now, because those who once made it home are no longer there. Some have gone to build homes of their own. Others have passed to "where beyond these voices there is peace." What makes home here is the love and understanding that are there. And that is what is going to make home for us by and by.

4. Finally, in this land of a clearer vision of Jesus, in this land of sweet fellowship, in this homelike land, we are going to go on working and growing unhampered by the infirmities that often beset us here. I used to come bounding in from the farm to have my

laughter hushed at the sight of the pain-drawn face of my mother. She sometimes suffered from terrible headaches. But now that she is gone, I love to think of her as in a land where the head doesn't ache any more, and where "health ever blossoms on the cheek and sparkles in the eye." In a land like this we can really "work for an age at a sitting, and never grow tired at all." Thus working we shall go on growing more and more into the likeness of our Lord.

What then shall we say of those dear to us who have passed into that unseen world? Surely we shall not grudge them their rest and their reward. I have a friend who recently lost a daughter that was beautiful in body as she was beautiful in soul. But, though the mother was a professing Christian, she took an attitude toward this experience that was entirely pagan. When I tried to comfort her, she turned upon me bitterly, telling me that her daughter had so much for which to live. What a strange and foolish attitude for one who is a Christian! If she had much for which to live here, surely she does not have less now that she has passed into the immediate presence of her Lord. Therefore, we are not to think of those who have gone to be with Christ as cheated, but as enriched forevermore.

Then what of us who are left behind? Sometimes the going of those we love leaves us so benumbed that we lose all interest in life. That, too, is an attitude that is un-Christian. It is unworthy of our Lord, it is unworthy of those who, though they have passed within the vale, still love us. I am thinking this beautiful Easter of my own father and mother. They have been gone for many years. But were they still here I am sure that they would have me face up to life in a gallant and Christlike fashion. Surely they yearn for this no less now that they have passed into that land where they no longer see as through a glass darkly, but face to face. Certainly those who await our coming would have us always at our golden best. Paul's faith makes this possible. Not only so, but it makes both life and death our friends. "For me to live is Christ, and to die is gain."